Berklee Practice Method

CELLO

Get Your Band Together

MATT GLASER
MIMI RABSON

and the
Berklee Faculty

Berklee Press

Editor in Chief: Jonathan Feist
Vice President of Online Learning and Continuing Education: Debbie Cavalier
Assistant Vice President of Berklee Media: Robert F. Green
Dean of Continuing Education: Carin Nuernberg
Editorial Assistants: Dominick DiMaria, Sarah Walk
Consulting Editor: Eugene Friesen

ISBN 978-0-87639-132-7

1140 Boylston Street
Boston, MA 02215-3693 USA
(617) 747-2146

Visit Berklee Press Online at
www.berkleepress.com

DISTRIBUTED BY

HAL•LEONARD®
CORPORATION
7777 W. BLUEMOUND RD. P.O. BOX 13819
MILWAUKEE, WISCONSIN 53213

Visit Hal Leonard Online at
www.halleonard.com

DESIGN TEAM

Matt Marvuglio	Curriculum Editor
	Dean of the Professional Performance Division
Jonathan Feist	Series Editor
Rich Appleman	Chair Emeritus of the Bass Department
Larry Baione	Chair of the Guitar Department
Eugene Friesen	Professor of Strings
Jeff Galindo	Assistant Professor of Brass
Matt Glaser	Artistic Director of the Center for American Roots Music
Russell Hoffmann	Associate Professor of Piano
Charles Lewis	Associate Professor of Brass
Jim Odgren	Professor of Woodwinds
Tiger Okoshi	Professor of Brass
Bill Pierce	Chair of the Woodwind Department
Tom Plsek	Chair of the Brass Department
Mimi Rabson	Associate Professor of Strings
John Repucci	Assistant Chair of the Bass Department
Ed Saindon	Professor of Percussion
Ron Savage	Chair of the Ensemble Department
Casey Scheuerell	Professor of Percussion
Paul Schmeling	Chair Emeritus of the Piano Department

The Band

Rich Appleman	Bass
Larry Baione	Guitar
Eugene Friesen	Cello
Jim Odgren	Saxophone
Mimi Rabson	Violin
Casey Scheuerell	Drums
Paul Schmeling	Keyboard

Music composed by Matt Marvuglio
Recording produced and engineered by Rob Jaczko, Chair of the Music Production and
    Engineering Department

Contents

CD Tracks

Foreword

Berklee College of Music has been training musicians for over fifty years. Our graduates go onto successful careers in the music business, and many have found their way to the very top of the industry, producing hit records, receiving the highest awards, and sharing their music with millions of people.

An important reason why Berklee is so successful is that our curriculum stresses the practical application of musical principles. Our students spend a lot of time playing together in bands. When you play with other musicians, you learn things that are impossible to learn in any other way. Teachers are invaluable, practicing by yourself is critical, but performing in a band is the most valuable experience of all. That's what is so special about this series: it gives you the theory you need, but also prepares you to play in a band.

The goal of the *Berklee Practice Method* is to present some of Berklee's teaching strategies in book and audio form. The chairs of each of our instrumental departments—guitar, bass, keyboard, percussion, woodwind, brass, and string—have gotten together and discussed the best ways to teach you how to play in a band. They teamed with some of our best faculty and produced a set of books with play-along audio tracks that uniquely prepares its readers to play with other musicians.

Students who want to study at Berklee come from a variety of backgrounds. Some have great technique, but have never improvised. Some have incredible ears, but need more work on their reading skills. Some have a very creative, intuitive sense of music, but their technical skills aren't strong enough, yet, to articulate their ideas.

The *Berklee Practice Method* teaches many of these different aspects of musicianship. It is the material that our faculty wishes all Berklee freshmen could master before arriving on our doorstep.

When you work through this book, don't just read it. You've got to play through every example, along with the recording. Better yet, play them with your own band.

Playing music with other people is how you will learn the most. This series will help you master the skills you need to become a creative, expressive, and supportive musician that anyone would want to have in their band.

Gary Burton
Executive Vice President,
Berklee College of Music

Preface

Thank you for choosing the *Berklee Practice Method* for cello. This book/CD package, developed by the faculty of Berklee College of Music, is part of the *Berklee Practice Method* series—the instrumental method that teaches how to play in a band.

The recording included with this method provides an instant band you can play along with, featuring great players from Berklee's performance faculty. Each tune has exercises and practice tracks that will help prepare you to play it. Rock, blues, and funk are just some of the styles you will perform.

The lessons in this book will guide you through technique that is specific to playing a cello in a contemporary ensemble. When you play in a band, your primary concern is with melody, improvising, playing the groove, and understanding chords. This is very different than traditional classical playing, and it will be a major part of this method. This book is intended for cellists who know how to read notes and basic rhythms, and play all major scales and some arpeggios. Ideally, this method should be learned under the guidance of a private teacher, but cello players learning on their own will also find it invaluable.

Most important, you will learn the skills you need to play cello in a band. Play along with the recording, and play with your friends. This series coordinates methods for many different instruments, and all are based on the same tunes, in the same keys. If you know a drummer, guitarist, horn player, etc., have them pick up the *Berklee Practice Method* for their own instruments, and then you can jam together.

Work hard, make music, have fun!

Matt Glaser, Artistic Director of the Center for American Roots Music
Mimi Rabson, Associate Professor of Strings
Berklee College of Music

Basics

Before you begin, you should understand the following topics.

PLUGGING IN

In a band, instruments are generally amplified. A device, such as a microphone or pickup, carries the sound to either an amplifier or a mixer.

In the past, a cellist's options for amplification were limited, but in recent years, the technology has come a long way, and you have a number of good choices: microphones, pickups, or electric cellos.

To protect your equipment and your ear drums, follow these steps when you use an amp or mixing board. It is similar for all kinds of electrification.

1. Turn off the amp and set the volume down to 0.

2. Plug your cable into your mic, pickup, or cello and then into the amp.

3. Turn on the amp.

4. If you are using a pickup or electric instrument, turn up your instrument's volume all the way.

5. Play at a medium volume. Slowly, turn up the amp or mixer volume until it is loud enough.

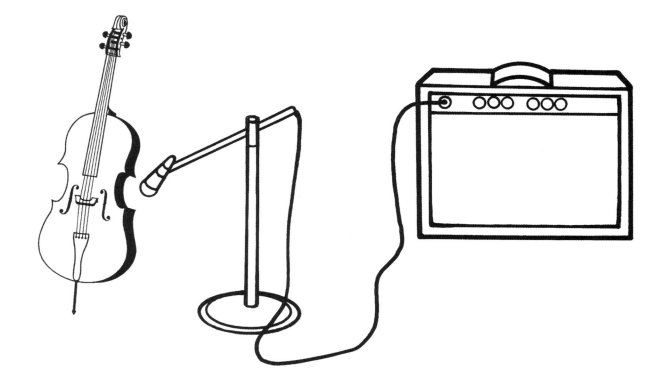

Microphones

Most varieties of microphones work well for cellos; a regular dynamic microphone will work fine. You can also use a "lavelier" mic that clips onto your cello. Better quality microphones will give you a better sound.

Some microphones need batteries, and some require "phantom power" from a mixer or preamplifier. Be sure you understand how your mic is powered, before you buy it.

What you need: A mic, an XLR cable, an XLR-to-1/4" converter, a mic stand (if it's not a stick-on mic), and an amplifier (or a sound system). Some mics require batteries or a "phantom power" source; check with your dealer regarding how your mic is powered.

Cost: $50 to $5000

Pros: It's easy, and you don't have to modify your acoustic cello.

Cons: There is a great danger of feedback, especially if you are playing with a loud band. Never point your mic at your amplifier or the sound system's speakers.

If you use a microphone, position it a few feet away from your instrument to get a warmer sound. Close miking will give you a rawer sound, which you may want for certain types of music.

Pickups

A pickup, or "transducer," transforms your strings' vibrations into an electronic signal. This signal can then be directed to an amplifier. Some pickups slip into the opening on the side of your bridge, some stick to the bridge, and some stick to the body of the instrument.

Some pickups are built into the bridge of the soundpost. These should be installed by a repair technician.

What you need: A pickup, a 1/4" cable (also called a "guitar cord"), and an amplifier. Some pickups come with their own cable.

Cost: $100 to $500 (plus installation, if needed)

Pros: It's easy, and there is less chance for feedback.

Cons: Your instrument may no longer sound like a cello. It may sound more like some kind of space sax with a cold. This can be corrected with a good pre-amp, amp, reverb, and other effects (see "amplifiers and effects" in the following sections).

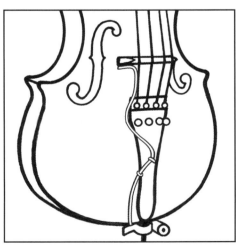

Electric Cellos

Guitar players have used electric instruments for decades. Electric cellos are similar. They have their pickups built in, so you can just plug them in and play. A *hollow body* electric cello can be used as an acoustic cello, if necessary. These instruments are prone to feedback. *Solid body* instruments require amplification, but they eliminate all possibility of feedback.

What you need: An electric cello, a 1/4" guitar cable, and an amplifier.

Cost: $350 to $3000

Pros: No feedback. Since the shape of the instrument is no longer necessary for sound production, there are some really cool-looking instruments out there that come in lots of colors. Also you can get 5- and 6-string instruments as well. Unplugged, these instruments are good for quiet practicing.

Cons: Again, the sound will not bring Stradivarius to mind, but many new sonic possiblities open up.

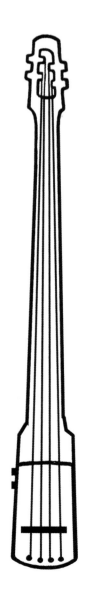

Other Gear

Once your sound is in an electric signal, various other pieces of gear will help you modify its volume level or timbre.

- **Amplifiers**

Amplifiers boost the volume of the electronic signal coming from your mic, pickup, or electric instrument. An amp will make the electronic signal loud enough to play in most situations. There are lots of amplifiers on the market, and since all electronic instruments use them, it's easy to find them used.

Once you have electrified your sound, take your cello to your local music store and have them show you around the amps. You'll notice most amps have some kind of tone controls: bass, treble, mid range, or maybe a more complex kind of equalization (EQ). These controls accentuate different frequencies of your sound. Try them out to get the sound you like the best. Often, the treble control needs to be turned way down, to get a warmer cello sound, and sometimes even small adjustments to the tone controls yield good results.

You can get a little amp that clips onto your belt for $35. The price goes up from there. A good amp that produces a fairly realistic cello sound will cost from $250 to $2500 new. Amps can be heavy, so you may want to get some kind of luggage rack to carry it around.

- **Volume pedals**

A volume pedal is a useful, though optional, piece of equipment. With a touch of your foot, it will allow you to get loud enough to play a solo, and then afterwards, come back down to ensemble volume. Or to suddenly go into a loud section after a quiet beginning. They cost $30 to $80 and are well worth it.

- **Effects**

Once you can actually be heard in your band, you may want to start altering your sound with distortion, reverb (short for "reverberation"), compression, pitch shifting, flanging, wah-wah, and so on. Cellists can use the same effects devices as those used by guitar players.

The list of things you can do is huge. There are "stomp boxes" that range in price from $50 to $200. Stomp boxes generally have one kind of effect, which you can control with a foot pedal. Other devices do what several stomp boxes would do, all in one machine. These are a little more expensive.

Some machines can be programmed to do what you tell them. There are pedal boards for the floor, devices that clip to your belt, and lately, some that you can plug into your computer that use effects stored on the Internet. Again, since guitarists use the same ones, most music stores have a number of effects devices for you to try.

Final Thoughts on Gear

The world of electronics is vast and fairly untapped by cellists. Ask fellow electric musicians what they are using. Get friendly with your local music store and keep up with what's new. There are several good magazines and catalogs that can keep you up to date with the latest sounds. If you don't like the sound you are getting, you can easily change it with a new EQ setting, a different amp, a new stomp box, or a new pickup. Explore!

This technology is always changing. Whatever you buy today, there will be a better one in six months that will probably cost less than what you paid for yours. Luckily, there is a large used market in the world of music electronics. The prices quoted here are for new gear, but there are lots of great buys to be had in the used market. And if you do buy new, you can usually sell your old gear and get some of your money back.

When you play using amplification, you will need to carry more gear around with you. Keep a couple of extra guitar cords and 9-volt batteries (for stomp boxes) in your case. You never know when one will stop working or someone else will need to borrow one.

Finally, remember your ears. Amplification lets you play loud, but you have to be careful. You only have one pair of ears, and if they get broken or damaged, you can't fix them. If you really have to play loud, use earplugs. Permanent hearing loss is a common problem among rock musicians.

Learning More

Though you won't generally find a variety of pickups and cellos at your local music store, they are gradually becoming more common. Check out various string-oriented magazines and Web sites for sources of dealers. School music teachers may have information about different publications or where to buy instruments and accessories.

PERFORMANCE HEALTH

Athletes rely on several kinds of specialists whose job it is to make sure that they are in peak physical condition. Coaches and trainers help them warm up before practice and cool down afterwards. If they get injured, they get benched until they are better.

Although playing music isn't football, it is a strenuous physical activity. Many talented people fall by the wayside because they don't take care of their bodies.

You have to be your own coach and make sure you are relaxed and warmed up before you play, and that you cool down sufficiently after you play. If you're in any pain, bench yourself. If the pain persists more than a couple of days, seek professional help. Too many people are out of the game before it starts because they didn't take care of themselves. Don't let that happen to you.

The best thing you can do to preserve your performance health is to maintain a healthy posture and hand position. This is one of the reasons why having a teacher is so important. A teacher, like an athlete's coach, will make sure that you are moving in a healthy way.

Self-taught string players are rare, and teaching effective cello technique is beyond the scope of this book. Keep in mind that good cello technique is tailored to the individual needs and size of the player. In other words, a private instructor will save a lot of time!

There are also a growing number of helpful, free tutorials online.

Sit forward in the chair with both feet on the floor. The shoulder of the cello should rest around the top of your rib cage so your knees cradle the widest portion of the cello below the bouts. The neck of the instrument will extend up to your left so the tuning pegs of the C and G strings are close to your left ear. Good cello technique includes keeping a straight line from your elbows to the knuckles of both hands. Since we rely on the weight of our arms and hands to achieve strain-free playing, keeping the elbows high and mobile will encourage good body balance above the instruments. As with good posture generally, keeping the head directly over the shoulders will help to avoid additional strain of the neck, shoulder, and back muscles.

HIGHER POSITIONS AND SHIFTING

Since we cellists need to shift positions to play many scales, we have to shift more than other string players. In this book, many examples are written low on the instrument in order to avoid shifting. Some exercises however require the use of higher positions, and of course you can play any of these exercises and tunes in any octave you like.

It can be really useful to draw a fingering chart so you have a visual "fretboard" in your mind as you move up and down by different intervals.

Cellists mostly use two hand positions: in non-extended position we play half-steps between each finger, in extended position we extend between our first and second fingers (marked as x1 or x2) to play a whole step.

Fingerings in this book will sometimes be clarified with the string on which the fingering should be used: I. for the A string, II. for the D string, III. for the G string, and IV. for the C string.

As you shift between positions, it's important to develop a habit of releasing the pressure of your hand on the fingerboard slightly to reduce friction.

CELLO IN A BAND

The cello can play several different roles in a band. It's a really effective bass instrument played either plucked (pizzicato) or bowed (arco). It's great at supplying inner harmony lines, or rhythmic energy to add power to the drums, bass, piano, and guitar. The cello has a beautiful harp-like quality when arpeggiating chords, and of course, we can play the melody too. This book will teach you many techniques you need to work with other musicians, and we mostly treat the cello as a melody instrument.

Because of the cello's low register, it's important that your bandmates listen to your parts and adjust their parts to keep the cello audible and clear. And it's also important to learn the higher positions on the cello so you can step into the brighter light of the high register when you need to.

TUNING

Before you play, tune your strings to the right notes. If your string is flat (too loose), tighten its tuning peg to raise the pitch. If your string is sharp (too tight), loosen its tuning peg to lower the pitch. As you get close to the right pitch, listen for *beats* (tiny waves of sound) as you play your note along with the correctly tuned note. Slight differences in pitch causes these audible beats. Keep tuning until you don't hear any beats.

There are many ways to tune. One of the most convenient is using an electric tuner. You can also tune by ear, using this recording.

Tuning to the *Berklee Practice Method* Recording

1. Listen to track 1, "Tuning Note A."

2. Play your A string. Determine whether the pitch of your A string is above or below the recorded pitch. Don't worry if you can't tell, at first. Just turn the A string's peg slowly, in either direction, until it sounds right.

3. While your string is still sounding its note, turn the A string's tuning peg until it is at the same pitch as the tuning note on the recording. Pluck it again every few seconds to keep it sounding its current pitch, until it is tuned.

4. When this string is tuned, tune the D, G, and C strings.

Your cello should now be in tune.

NOTATION

Notes are written on a staff.

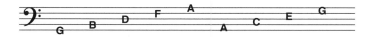

Cello music is usually written using the "bass clef" staff. Here are the notes for the lines and spaces in bass clef.

Ledger Lines

The staff can be extended with ledger lines.

ACCIDENTALS

Accidentals are symbols appearing before notes, showing that a pitch is raised or lowered for the duration of the measure, unless otherwise indicated.

♭	Flat	Next note down (half step)
♯	Sharp	Next note up (half step)
♮	Natural	Cancels a flat or sharp

SCALES: MAJOR AND MINOR

Scales are patterns of notes, presented sequentially in a single octave. Two common types of scales are the major and minor scales.

KEY SIGNATURES

Key signatures indicate a tune's key and show which notes always get sharps or flats. Accidentals on the lines and spaces in the key signature affect those notes unless there is a natural sign. Here are some key signatures used in this book.

RHYTHMS

Here are some basic rhythms. When there are no actual pitches, as in a clapping exercise, rhythms may be shown on the *percussion clef*. (The beats are numbered below the staff.)

Connect notes using a tie. The first note is held for a total of six beats.

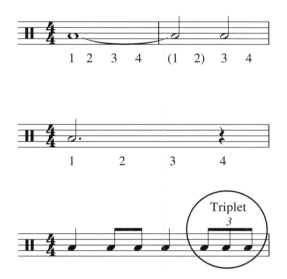

RHYTHMIC NOTATION

Music that just shows rhythms may be written in rhythmic notation. This is common for rhythm exercises when you clap or tap your foot, without sounding any specific pitches.

MEASURES

Groups of beats are divided into measures. Measure lenghts are shown with *time signatures*.
This measure is in $\frac{4}{4}$ time; there are four quarter notes in the measure.

In $\frac{12}{8}$ time, there are twelve eighth notes per measure.

ARTICULATIONS

Articulations give more information about how to play a note. Here are four common ones used in this book:

>	Accent	Loud
.	Staccato	Short
^	Short accent	Short and loud
–	Long	Hold for full value

Now, let's play!

SHIFTING

Shifting is the technique that string players use to move their hands up and down the fingerboard. Several of the excercises in this book require the ability to shift as denoted by the fingerings that are written above the notes. If you haven't learned to shift yet, we suggest you find a teacher to work with you to ensure that you develop the best possible technique.

"Sweet" is a *rock* tune. Rock started in the 1960s and has roots in blues, swing, r&b, and rock 'n' roll. There are many different styles of rock. To hear more rock, listen to artists such as Rage Against the Machine, Melissa Etheridge, Korn, Paula Cole, Bjork, Tori Amos, Primus, Jimi Hendrix, and Led Zeppelin.

LESSON 1
TECHNIQUE/THEORY

Listen to "Sweet" on the recording. The cello and saxophone play the melody together. Use of the "distortion" effect gives the cello sound a hard-rock edge. This tune has two parts.

In the first part of the melody, the cellist plays these notes. Use your ear to find the rhythms.

In the second part, the cello plays these notes.

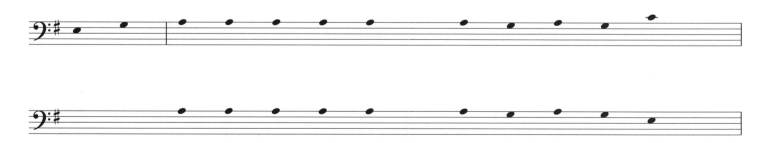

Play along with the recording, and try to match the melody. Notice that there is a short introduction before the first part begins.

Melodies such as "Sweet" are created out of different *licks*—short, melodic figures or *phrases*. A musical phrase is similar to a phrase in spoken or written language. It is a continuous musical idea that is unbroken and uninterrupted by long rests or periods of silence. Phrases can be short licks, or they can be extended melodies.

In "Sweet," the cello and lead guitar play the melody, and the other instruments play other kinds of parts. The parts all sound good together because the melody, the *chords* (three or more notes sounded together), and the *groove* (rhythmic time feel) all work together.

ARTICULATION

Articulation is the way a note is played—short, long, accented, and so on. Choosing good articulations for your notes and phrases will make your melodies come alive.

On a cello, different articulations are played by changing the way you use your bow. Changing the way you *attack* (start) and *release* (stop) the sound changes the note's articulation.

Legato

Notes in the first part of "Sweet" flow together smoothly. This is *legato* style articulation, often notated with a *slur* marking (⌣). Each note is held for its *full rhythmic value* so that it leads right up to the next note. Though cellists use slurs to indicate bowings, other instruments use them to indicate phrasing, so try to determine who added the slurs to the notation and why. They may or may not make sense as bowings.

When you play legato notes, try to minimize the space between the notes. You can do this by playing all the notes in one bow or by making smooth bow changes between the notes.

Practice legato long tones with the recording. Only change bows every two measures, where you see a comma (Ꞌ). Count in your head while you play, and make sure you hold each note for its full value. Then try a smooth bow change on each note.

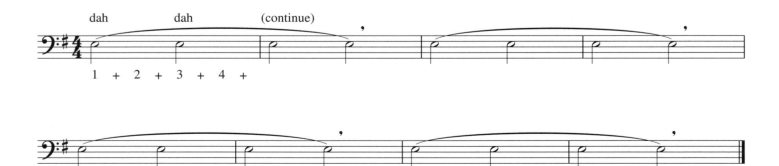

Practice the first part of "Sweet" using legato articulation, using the same track. The notes within each phrase should sound connected. What bowings would you use to make them legato?

Staccato

Notes in the second part to "Sweet" are much shorter and more separated. The opposite of legato (long) is *staccato* (short). Staccato notes are indicated with a dot (·). To play staccato, use separate bows for each note. Use the middle or upper half of the bow for more control of your articulation, and to avoid the more classical style of staccato used in classical music. Make a little accent at the beginning of each note by pressing with the index finger of your bow hand. Make a clean release at the end of each note in the same way.

Staccato notes are not held for their full rhythmic value, and there should be space between notes. Staccato quarter notes are written like this:

These notes sound much shorter than quarter notes—more like sixteenths. Here is the same line written as sixteenth notes. As you can see, the dots are much easier to read than the sixteenth-note flags with dotted-eighth-note rests.

Practice staccato articulations with the recording, one note per beat. Though the notes are short, you should still think about phrasing—that is, "musicalize" groups of two or four bars using dynamics.

LISTEN **4** PLAY

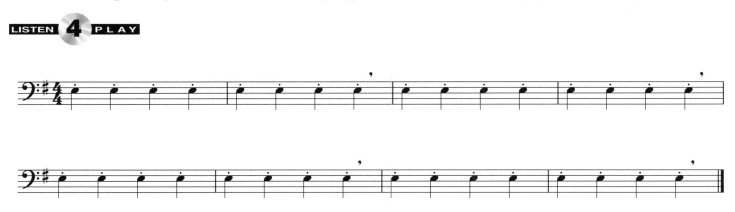

Now practice staccato eighth notes with the recording. Try this in two different ways.

1. The first time you play this exercise, keep your bow on the string the whole time, using the upper half of the bow, near the balance point of the bow.

2. The second time, "brush" the string with the bow, lifting it on either side of the note.

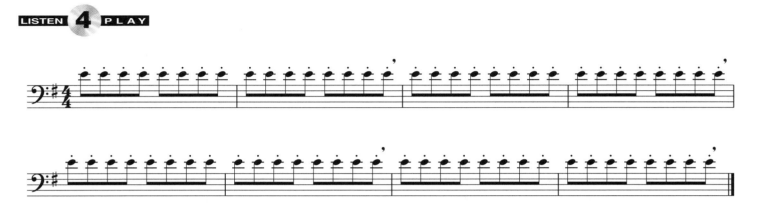

The licks in the second part of "Sweet" each have three notes that are played staccato on the recording. The other notes shouldn't be as short. Practice these licks a few times to get the staccato feel, and then practice it with the recording.

PRACTICE TIP

Keep your bow on the string, except during rests. If you play a combination of short and long notes, this makes it much easier to play accurate rhythms and stay in the groove.

LEAD SHEETS

Articulations may be marked in formal, published music. When you play in a band, more often, you will use informal music that only shows chord symbols and melody, usually with no articulations, no phrasing, and no other expressive markings. This is called a *lead sheet*. Finding the right articulations will be up to you.

This is what the first part to "Sweet" looks like on a lead sheet.

The whole band may read the same lead sheet. Each player will use it differently to create a part for their instrument. As a cello player, one way you will use the lead sheet is to read and play the song's melody.

The keyboard, guitar, and bass all play parts using notes from the chords. By tuning in to the chords, you'll find it easier to keep your place in the music. When it's your turn to *solo* (improvise), the chord symbols will be useful to you as well, as we will see in later chapters.

Different bands will create different parts for the same tune. This is one of the coolest things about lead-sheet notation: it leaves room for individual interpretation.

You will see the full lead sheet to "Sweet" in lesson 4.

Lead sheets will rarely be written in bass clef, so until you are comfortable transposing down an octave (an invaluable skill for creative and collaborative musicians), you may want to try writing your own lead sheet in bass clef.

LESSON 2
LEARNING THE GROOVE

WHAT IS A GROOVE?

A *groove* is a combination of musical patterns in which everyone in the band feels and plays to a common pulse. This creates a sense of unity and momentum. The *rhythm section* (usually drums, bass, guitar, and keyboard) lays down the groove's dynamic and rhythmic feel. A cellist or other soloist also contributes to the groove and performs the melody based on this feel.

Listen to "Sweet." As is common in hard rock, the groove to "Sweet" has a strong, clear pulse, and a loud, forceful sound. The drums play a heavy, repetitive beat. The bass outlines the harmonic structure. The rhythm guitar and keyboard play chords. The cello and lead guitar play the melody. Everyone uses the same rhythms, though often at different times. This makes the whole band sound like one unit; they're all *hooked up* with the groove.

LISTEN **2** PLAY

In lesson 1, when you played along with the recording and matched the cello part, you hooked up with a groove and became part of the band.

Cello in a Groove

On our recording of "Sweet," the cellist has two roles in the groove: melody and improvisation. If there were several cellos, or other strings, there might be a third kind of role: that of a member of a string section. In a section, the strings may play chords together, or they may all play the same melody in *unison* (at the same time). In a smaller band, like the one on our recording, there is only one cello player. This player is *out front*, and at the center of attention.

Rock music has included strings for a long time. Bands such as the Beatles used them back in the 1960s. In those days, strings were generally used more in the backgrounds of rock bands, rather than up front. With technology such as electric violins and better pickups, strings are becoming more common in the rock scene.

HOOKING UP TO ROCK

As a cellist, though you are not a member of the rhythm section, you are still part of the groove and must tap into its rhythmic feel. The way you play should help the other band members feel the beat or pulse you feel.

The way to hook up to a groove is by learning its unique pulse and rhythmic feel. Then, your playing will hook up rhythmically with the rest of the band. Your phrasing and articulation will help you define the rhythms of the melody and hook up to the groove.

The best thing to do is to latch on to one of the parts in the rhythm section: bass, keyboard, or even just the snare drum. Imitate its sound and feel as you play.

> **PRACTICE TIP**
>
> Use clear bow strokes. Think about the beginnings and the endings of each note you play. Play each note like a snare drum hit.

Count along with the beat, repeating "1, 2, 3, 4" through every measure. While you count, play a very short note along with the snare drum on the *backbeat*—beats 2 and 4, where you see the circles below. A strong backbeat is one of the characteristics of rock grooves.

> **PRACTICE TIP**
>
> To create a good percussive sound while working on these rhythm exercises, try dropping your bow on the string near the frog while muting the strings with the left hand. The "chops" require a little practice, and there are multiple tutorials available on DVD and/or online. They work best on the lower strings. Try not to sound a particular pitch; it should be more like a snare drum hit. The more you control the drop, the better your rhythm will be.

LISTEN 3 PLAY

While you "chop" and count, tap your foot on the quarter-note pulse.

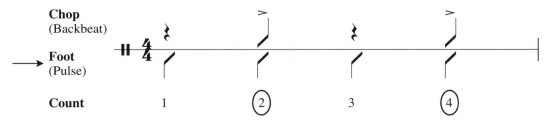

This tune has a sixteenth-note feel, so change your counting to sixteenth notes, matching the cymbals. On each beat, count evenly, "1 e + a, 2 e + a, 3 e + a, 4 e + a" (say "and" for "+"). Try saying this first at a slower tempo, without the recording, until you get the hang of it. When you are ready, play the recording and say the syllables in tempo.

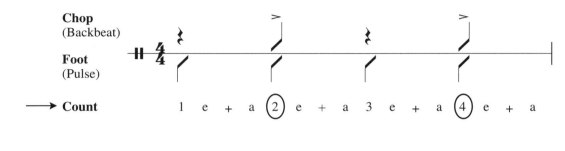

LISTEN 3 PLAY

Play the rhythm of the cello's first part to "Sweet" using only the note E (first finger on the D string). Tap your foot on the quarter note, and feel the sixteenth-note *subdivisions* (divisions within a beat). When you are ready, do this along with the recording. The same phrase is played twice. Try singing the melody along with the CD at the same time.

Play E
(Melody Rhythms)

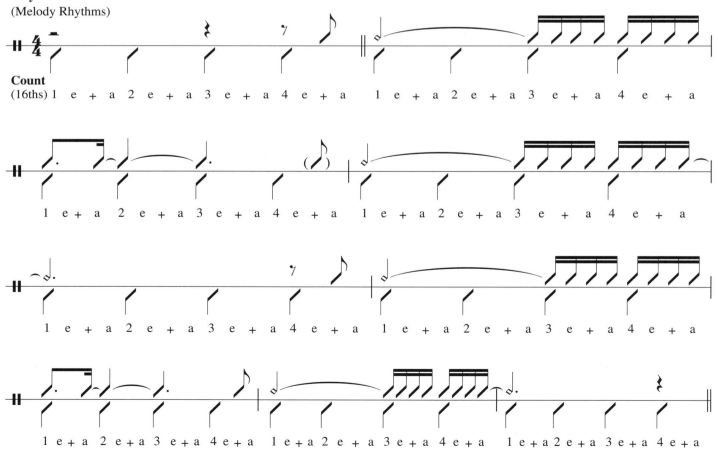

Play the actual part along with the recording. Tap your foot, and feel the sixteenth notes as you play. Use legato articulations, and hook up with the groove.

Listen to the second part to "Sweet," find the pulse, and count along. When you are ready, play an open A along with the recording. The same rhythmic lick repeats, played a total of eight times.

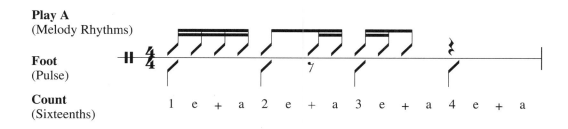

Play the actual part along with the recording. Tap your foot and count in your head as you play. Watch your articulations, and hook up with the groove.

Finally, play both parts of the melody, following your ear and not looking at the music. Make sure to use different articulations on each part, and hook up with the rhythm section. When the cello solos, sit back and listen, and continue to feel the groove. Come in again when the melody returns.

LESSON 3
IMPROVISATION

Improvisation is the invention of a solo. When you improvise, you tell the story of what you think about the tune, and what it means to you. Though an improvised solo may seem spontaneous to the audience, the musician probably did a lot of preparation before performing it. There are three things you must know before you start improvising: the song melody, when you should solo, and what notes will sound good in your solo.

FORM AND ARRANGEMENT

When you are preparing to improvise on a tune, start by learning how it is organized. This will let you know when you should start your improvised solo and where the chords change.

Listen to "Sweet" and follow the cello. After an introduction by the rhythm section, the cello plays the melody. Then, there is an improvised cello solo. Finally, the cello plays the melody again, followed by a short ending.

During the improvised solo, you can still feel the written melody. That's because the improvisation follows the same chords as the written melody. This repeating chord structure is the same throughout the entire tune, and is called the song's *form*—its plan or structure.

A common way to show this organization is with a *chord chart*. Chord charts don't show rhythm or pitch, just measures and chord symbols. The slash marks (*/ / / /*) mean "play in time."

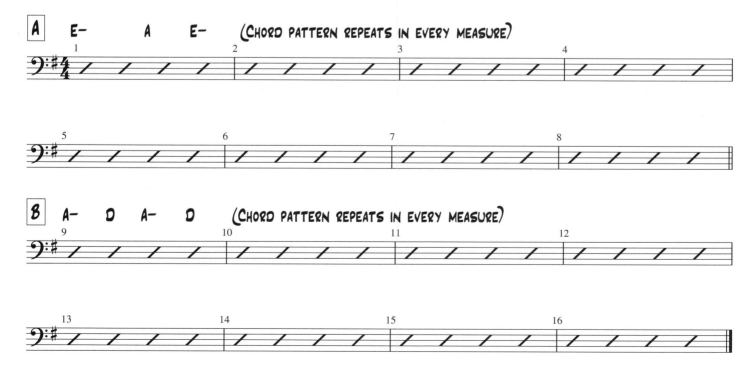

The chord chart makes it easy to see that the form of "Sweet" is sixteen measures long. It has two primary musical ideas: the first eight measures present the first idea (Idea "A"), with the E– A E– patterns. The second eight measures present the second idea (Idea "B"), with the A– D A– D patterns. This form can be described simply as "AB" or "AB form." These letters help us remember the form, freeing us from having to read while we're performing.

HEAD/CHORUS

One complete repetition of this form is called a *chorus*. A chorus can feature the written melody, in which case it is called the *head*, or it can feature just the chord structure, supporting an improvisation. The word *chorus* is also used to mean a song section that is alternated with varying verses. In this book, however, the word "chorus" is only used to mean "once through the form."

ARRANGING "SWEET"

Your band can choose how many choruses you want to play, and create your own *arrangement* of "Sweet." The number of choruses depends on how many players will improvise when you perform the tune. On the recorded performance of "Sweet," only one player solos (the cellist), playing for two choruses. Often, several members of the band will take turns playing choruses of improvised solos. A solo can be one or two choruses, or even more.

On the recording, the same basic arrangement is used for all the tunes: the head, an improvised cello solo, and then the head again. There are often short introductions and endings as well.

Listen to "Sweet" and follow the arrangement. This is the arrangement for "Sweet" played on the recording:

LISTEN **2** PLAY

INTRO	HEAD	CELLO SOLO: 2X	HEAD	ENDING
4 MEASURES	1 CHORUS = 16 MEASURES	1 CHORUS = 16 MEASURES	1 CHORUS = 16 MEASURES	2 MEASURES

When you play "Sweet" with your band, you can play your own arrangement, adding extra solo choruses, different endings, or other changes.

IDEAS FOR IMPROVISING

When you improvise, some notes will sound better than others. There are many ways to find notes that will sound good. You can use the notes from the tune's melody, you can use notes from the chords, and you can use notes from scales that match the tune. Eventually, this becomes intuitive, and you can just follow your ear.

Scales: E Minor Pentatonic

The cellist on this recording of "Sweet" built much of the solo using notes from a *pentatonic scale*. Pentatonic scales are among the simplest and most versatile types of scales in all of music. All pentatonic scales have five notes. There are two common types of pentatonic scales: major and minor. For "Sweet," the soloist used the *minor pentatonic scale* built on E. This scale works well here because the tune is in the key of E minor. Notice that the E is repeated, up an octave, to close the scale.

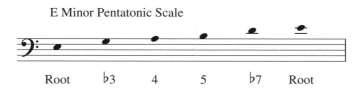

Use this scale to create your improvised licks. You only need a few notes to create a lick, so divide the scale into halves. Use one half for some licks and the other half for other licks. This will add contrast between them.

Here are some of the licks that can be created using some notes from these groups.

You may have noticed that all of these licks use the same rhythm. This is the rhythm used above.

Plugging different notes into the same rhythm is another good technique for building solos. It makes the licks sound related, like part of the same thing. You don't need to use the same exact rhythm every time, but some repetition can be very effective.

CALL AND RESPONSE

Listen to each phrase, and then play it back, echoing it exactly. Each lick comes from the E minor pentatonic scale, using the groupings and the rhythm discussed above. Slashes ("/") in measures marked "play" mean that you should play in time during those measures. Listen carefully, and hook up with the groove.

LISTEN 5 PLAY

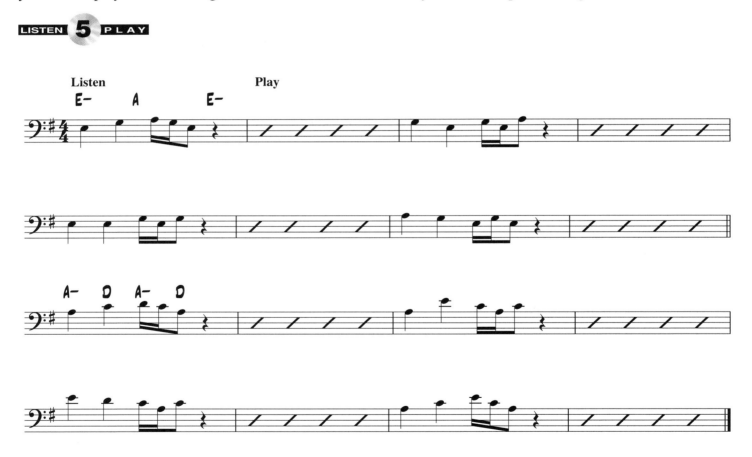

Keep practicing that track until you can echo all phrases perfectly. Then do the same thing for the phrases on this next track.

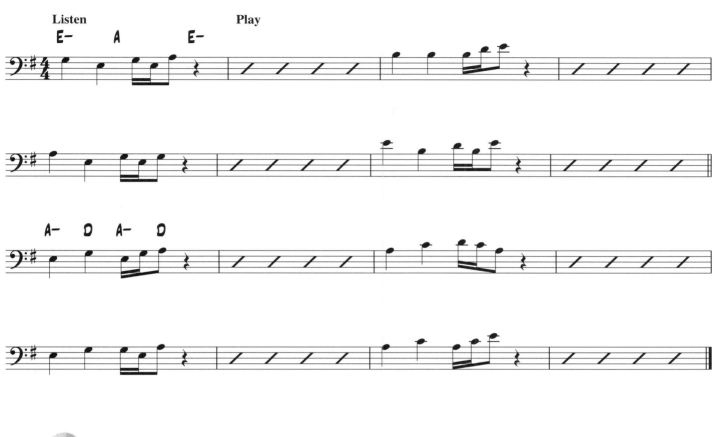

Play the same two tracks again. This time, instead of echoing the phrases exactly, answer them with your own improvised phrases. Use the same rhythms, and only use notes of the E minor pentatonic scale.

Write out some of your own licks, like the ones you have been playing. Don't worry about perfecting your notation; just sketch out your ideas. This will help you remember them when you are improvising.

PRACTICE TIP

A good solo combines two elements: rhythmic drive and melodic content. Combine that with your unique musical personality, and you've got it.

 **LISTEN 7 PLAY**

Create a 1-chorus solo using any techniques you have learned. Memorize your solo, and practice it along with the recording.

PLAY IN A BAND TIP

When playing in a band, listen to the other players' parts, and try to create a musical conversation. This makes playing much more fun, and more musical too. When you are improvising a solo, listen to what the other instruments are playing. They will suggest many ideas that you can use in your solo, such as rhythms and licks, and you will inspire each other. When someone else is soloing, try to find a place in the rhythm section by imitating the rhythm players and using those percussive "chops."

LESSON 4
READING

When you play in a band, sometimes you will get a cello part that shows exactly what you should play. Other times, you may get a lead sheet, giving you more freedom to create your own part. You should be able to play from either one.

CELLO PART

Below is a written cello part to "Sweet." This part shows articulation markings and rehearsal letters.

HARD ROCK   Style indication. This tune is hard rock, and you should play it in that style: heavy bass, strong beat, sixteenth-note feel, and other elements typical of that hard-edged sound.

$\downarrow = 86$ Metronome marking. This tells you how fast you should play this tune. If you have a metronome, set it to 86, and play "Sweet" at that tempo.

INTRO   Introduction. The written part begins with an introduction, which is made up of four measures of the B section.

3   A bar with a number over it means that you should rest for that number of measures. The introduction begins with just the rhythm section, so you can sit out. But count along, so you are ready to come in on the pickup to letter A.

A   Rehearsal letter. These are different than form letters, which you saw in lesson 3. These letters help you when you are practicing with other musicians because everyone's parts have the same letters marked at the same places.

||: :|| Repeat signs. Play the music between these signs twice (or more).

A9   Rehearsal letter with measure number. These mark different areas within a chorus. Again, this can be helpful during rehearsals.

AFTER SOLOS, REPEAT TO ENDING   When the soloists are finished, play the head one more time, and then proceed to the measures marked "Ending."

ENDING   A final section that is added to the form. End the tune with these measures.

Play "Sweet" along with the recording. Follow the cello part exactly as it is written.

SWEET

Cello

By Matt Marvuglio

TIP

Sometimes, slurs are phrasing marks, not bowings. Change bowings as needed, especially when you are the only one playing the part. Use bowings to match the sound of the phrasing.

LEAD SHEET

Lead sheets present the chords and melody. Lead sheets give you more interpretive freedom than full formal cello parts do. Notice that there is no written introduction on this lead sheet. The introduction you hear in the recording is an interpretation of the lead sheet by that band. Your band should create your own unique arrangement.

Though actual cello parts are written in bass and tenor clef, lead sheets are nearly always in treble clef. It's a good idea to get used to seeing melodies in treble clef while playing them one or two octaves lower on cello.

SWEET

BY MATT MARVUGLIO

PLAY IN A BAND TIP

As you rehearse "Sweet," follow the lead sheet. It will help you keep your place in the form.

DAILY PRACTICE ROUTINE

ARTICULATION PRACTICE

Legato

Practice these two legato exercises along with the recording to the first part of "Sweet." Change your bow only where you see the breath marks. The notes should sound almost connected to each other.

> ### PRACTICE TIP
> Keep your bow on the string all the time. Try to make the changes of bow smooth by keeping your bow hand very flexible.

Legato Exercise 1

Legato Exercise 2

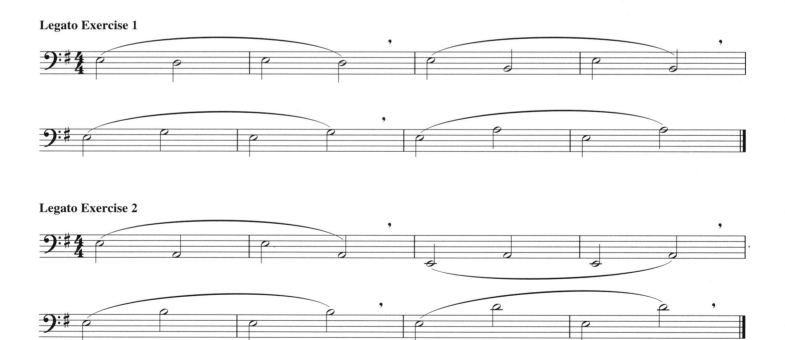

Staccato

Practice the E minor pentatonic scale along with the recording, using staccato articulations. Listen to the drums, and try to play your notes exactly in time.

LISTEN **4** PLAY

Staccato Exercise 1

Staccato Exercise 2

SCALE PRACTICE

Here are the notes of the E minor pentatonic scale through two octaves. When you are comfortable playing all of these notes, you'll be able to use them when you improvise.

In lesson 3, you divided the scale into two groups of three notes. There are other ways to group notes of this scale. For example, you can take groups of four consecutive scale notes, beginning on any scale degree. This next exercise shows you many different ways of grouping notes, and helps you master the E minor pentatonic scale throughout the cello's register. Practice it with both legato and staccato phrasing. This exercise is based on the form of "Sweet," so you can practice it along with the full track, playing it several times. Begin after the introduction.

IMPROVISATION PRACTICE

This exercise will help you practice improvising. You will use groups of notes from the E minor pentatonic scale and a rhythmic pattern, just like you did in lesson 3. The difference is that now you will be creating improvised licks while the music is playing.

Before you play, you must do two things. First, you must choose your groups of notes. For now, we'll use the same groups from lesson 3.

Second, you must choose a rhythmic figure. Again, we'll start with the one from lesson 3.

Here's how it works. You will be improvising with the rhythm section. In odd measures, you will play; in even measures, you will plan. When you plan, decide what you will play, choosing what notes to use in the rhythm above, choosing notes alternately from groups 1 and 2. Before you begin, plan your first measure. It will be organized like this:

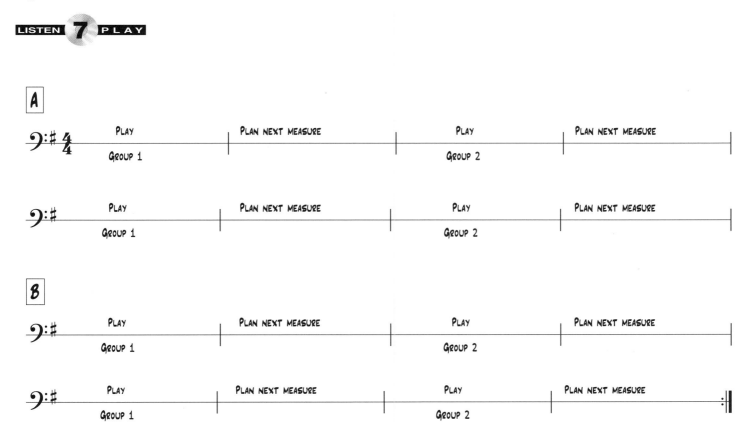

When you are comfortable with that, use different groups of notes and different rhythms. For groups of notes, choose some from the pentatonic exercise earlier in this section. For rhythms, you can use any of these, or write your own. Just keep it simple, and be strict in following it.

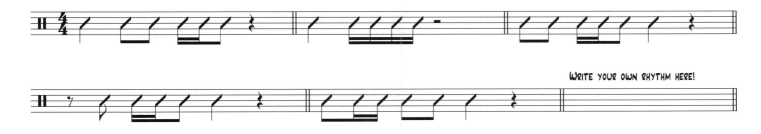

CHALLENGE

Choose different rhythms or note groups for the A section and for the B section. When you play along with the track, play the melody at the first and last chorus, as it is played on the recording.

SOLO PRACTICE

LISTEN **7** PLAY

Practice this solo along with the recording. Notice that much of it is based on the E minor pentatonic scale. If this solo is too high for you, write the high parts down an octave, or, better yet, create a solo that's comfortable for you.

MEMORIZE

LISTEN **7** PLAY

Memorizing the licks and melodies from these exercises will help you play the tune, especially when you improvise. What you practice helps you when you perform. But performing is the best practice, so get together with some other musicians and learn these tunes with your own band.

Memorize the cello part to "Sweet." Also memorize the lead sheet. The "Summary" shows everything you need to play "Sweet" from a lead sheet. Memorizing it will help you memorize the tune.

PRACTICE TIP
Write out your own exercises based on the E minor pentatonic scale. The more ways you find to make melodies from that scale, the more you make music that's truly your own!

SUMMARY

FORM	ARRANGEMENT	HARMONY	SCALE
16-BAR AB	INTRO: 4 M.		
(1 CHORUS = 16 BARS)	1 CHORUS MELODY		
A: 8 M.	2 CHORUS SOLO	A E− A B A− D	E MINOR PENTATONIC
B: 8 M.	1 CHORUS MELODY		
	END: 2 M.		

PLAY "SWEET" WITH YOUR OWN BAND!

"Do It Now" is a *blues* tune. Blues began in the late 1800s, and it has had a profound influence on American music styles, including rock, jazz, and soul. To hear more blues, listen to artists such as B.B. King, the Blues Brothers, Robben Ford, Bonnie Raitt, James Cotton, Albert King, and Paul Butterfield.

LESSON 5
TECHNIQUE/THEORY

Listen to the recording of "Do It Now" and play along. Try to match the cello. The melody has three lines. Each starts differently but ends the same.

LISTEN **8** PLAY

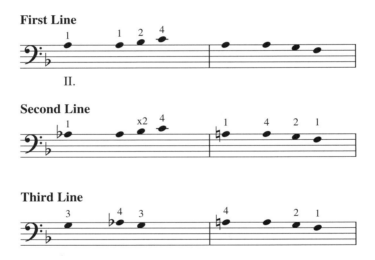

PRACTICE TIP

In melodies, look for patterns—notes that are the same or similar from one phrase to the next. In "Do It Now," the three phrases end exactly the same. Also, the first two phrases are very similar, with the only difference being that the first A-natural in the first phrase changes to an A-flat in the second. As you learn songs, notice what remains the same and what's different. You'll learn them faster.

SLIDES

Articulations, such as slides, can help you get a good blues sound in your playing.

If you listen to great blues singers, you may notice that they slide into some notes and slide off of other notes. Sometimes, they slide around a bunch of notes while singing just one syllable. This is called "melismatic singing." To get this sound on the cello, practice sliding into some notes and off of others.

Play along with the following track, and try to imitate the exact sound and length of the slides.

LISTEN **9** PLAY

LESSON 6
LEARNING THE GROOVE

HOOKING UP TO A BLUES SHUFFLE

LISTEN 8 PLAY

Listen to "Do It Now." This groove has its roots in traditional r&b, gospel, and jazz. The feel is often called a *12/8 shuffle* because of the twelve eighth notes in each bar. (The drums play these on the ride cymbal or hi-hat.)

Tap your foot on every beat, and count triplets: "1 trip-let 2 trip-let 3 trip-let 4 trip-let." The basic pulse (tap) is on the quarter note. However, each pulse also has an underlying triplet that divides the beat into three equal parts.

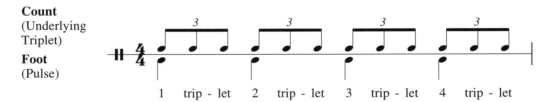

This triplet feel is part of what makes the beat a *shuffle*. While all shuffles don't include triplets on every single beat, the underlying triplet *feel* is always present.

The triplet is a fundamental aspect of all swing and shuffle beats. Understanding and feeling the concept of "subdivisions" (dividing the pulse into smaller rhythms) will help you play many other kinds of grooves.

"Do It Now" begins with the drums playing two beats of triplets. This establishes the shuffle groove. Listen for the steady triplet beat in the hi-hat, and find the triplet patterns in the other instruments. Listen to the bass part. Which beats have a triplet feel? Is the triplet pattern the same in every measure or does it change?

SWING EIGHTH NOTES

Eighth notes in shuffle grooves are usually played as triplets, even though they are notated as *straight* eighth notes.

Though these rhythms look different, in some musical styles, they are played the same. The notated part to "Do It Now" shows eighth notes notated like this:

Since it is a shuffle tune, they are played more like this:

The part is easier to read without the triplet markings on every beat, and the rhythms are played as triplets even though they are notated as if they were regular eighth notes. Interpreting rhythms in this way is called "swinging the eighth notes." Swing eighth notes are common in many styles of music, including blues, jazz, and swing.

Sometimes, the word "swing," "swing feel," or "shuffle" appears on the lead sheet, telling you how to play eighth notes. If there is no such indication, try it both ways and choose which fits the groove best. The style of the tune may help you choose whether to swing your eighth notes or play them straight.

Listen again to "Do It Now," and play the cello part along with the recording. Feel the triplets on every beat, listen to the drums, and hook up with the groove.

LESSON 7
IMPROVISATION

Listen to "Do It Now," and follow the form. The form of this tune is called a *12-bar blues*.

LISTEN **8** PLAY

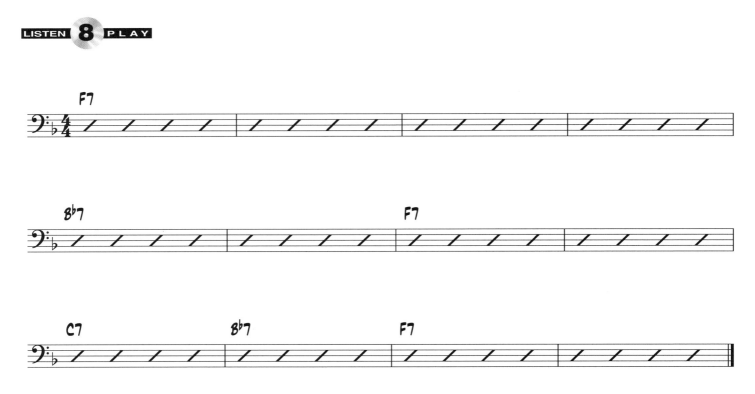

A 12-bar blues has three 4-bar phrases. It is common for the first two phrases in the melody to be similar and the third one to be different. This form is very common in many styles of music, including jazz, rock, and funk.

In "Do It Now," the first phrase has four bars of the I chord (F7). The second phrase has two bars of the IV chord (B♭7) followed by two bars of the I chord (F7). The third section has one bar of V (C7), one bar of IV (B♭7), and then two bars of I (F7). This is typically the way that chords move in blues.

Memorize the blues form and chord progression. You will see it again many times throughout your career.

About the Blues

The blues is the great aquifer that underlies all American music. Jazz, rock 'n' roll, country, and r&b are all continually fed by this giant river called the blues. If you're going to play any kind of popular music, you'll have to get used to playing the blues.

The blues is many things. In general, it's the expression of a sad feeling or playing music to make that sad feeling better. It's also a musical form, as discussed above. In vocal versions of the blues, the first two lyric lines are usually the same, and the third is different.

> *I'm gonna' buy myself a brand new pair of shoes.*
> *I'm gonna' buy myself a brand new pair of shoes.*
> *I'm gonna' quit singing those doggone hard-time blues.*

Here's a way to generalize about this form:

> *The second phrase of the blues is the same as the first.*
> *The second phrase of the blues is the same as the first.*
> *The third phrase of the blues is almost the same as the first.*

ARRANGEMENT

"Do It Now" begins with the drum playing two beats of triplets. This is called a *pickup*—a short introduction, less than a measure long, that leads to a strong downbeat. Here is the arrangement played on the recording.

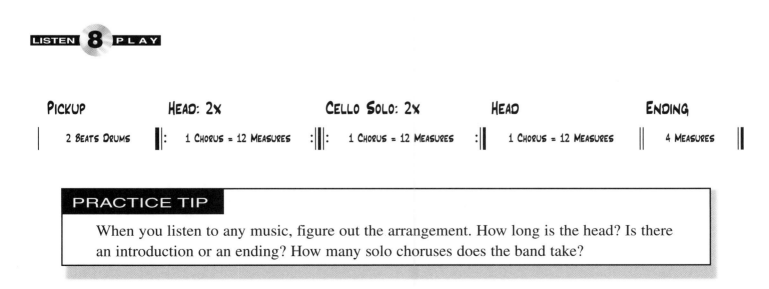

LISTEN **8** PLAY

PICKUP	HEAD: 2x	CELLO SOLO: 2x	HEAD	ENDING
2 BEATS DRUMS	‖: 1 CHORUS = 12 MEASURES :‖	‖: 1 CHORUS = 12 MEASURES :‖	1 CHORUS = 12 MEASURES ‖	4 MEASURES ‖

PRACTICE TIP

When you listen to any music, figure out the arrangement. How long is the head? Is there an introduction or an ending? How many solo choruses does the band take?

SCALES: F BLUES SCALE

In chapter 1, you created licks using the E minor pentatonic scale. Here is the F minor pentatonic scale:

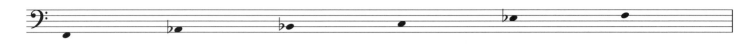

The *F blues scale* has just one more note—the flat fifth degree (B-natural):

Practice the notes of the F blues scale over the range of your cello. Extend it, if you can.

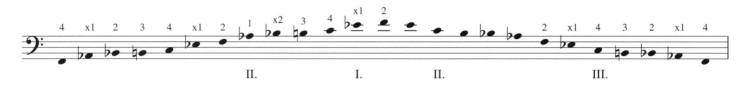

CALL AND RESPONSE

In these call-and-response exercises, divide the F blues scale into two groups. The B-natural will be used in both groups. The first chorus draws from group 1, and the second chorus draws from group 2. The notes of each group can be played in any octave.

Use this rhythm for each lick.

1. Echo each lick exactly as you hear it.
2. Improvise an answer to each lick. Use the same rhythm for each answer, but choose your own notes.

Use notes from group 1 in this chorus.

Listen   Play

Use notes from group 2 in this chorus.

Use notes from groups 1 or 2 in this chorus, choosing the same group as you hear on the recording.

Practice playing "Do It Now" using just the chord roots, and get the feel of the form. Memorize the blues form and chord progression. You will see it again many times throughout your career.

Chord tones—especially the root and fifth—are often the primary notes of a bass line, and they are connected by scale tones. You learned the chords of "Do It Now" in lesson 1. Now, you will learn a new scale that will help you connect these chord tones and create a good bass line.

Here is the first lick of "Do It Now." Notice how the **F7** chord tones, F and E♭, are placed prominently, one on the first beat and the other held for a long duration. The chord tones E♭ and C are connected by two notes from the F blues scale, B♭ and B-natural:

At a new chord symbol, play the new chord root on the first beat:

At the **B♭7** chord, there are notes that come from the *B♭ blues scale*—E♭ and E-natural, as well as chord tones. The other blues scale you might use is the C blues scale, though in the recording, the bass part stays on the root of this chord when it gets there:

PASSING TONES

Another idea for your bass lines is connect two notes using half steps. These in-between notes are called *chromatic notes* or *passing tones*. In fact, in the blues scale, the flat fifth is like a passing tone between the fourth and fifth notes of a minor pentatonic scale.

Passing tones help connect notes. In "Do It Now," the bass uses passing tones to connect the E♭ of the **F7** chord to the C of the **C** chord (measure 8 to 9):

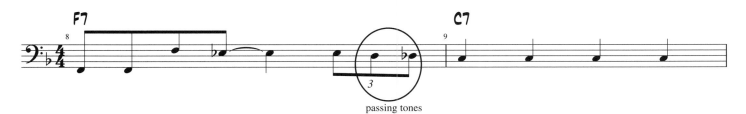

The D and D♭ passing tones don't fit the blues scales or chord tones of this tune, but they sound good here because they are tucked in between two chord tones. They are played quickly, on a weak beat, so they don't stand out. Their presence helps connect the two different chords, and gives the bass line more character.

Write out a few of your own ideas. Use notes from the F blues scale.

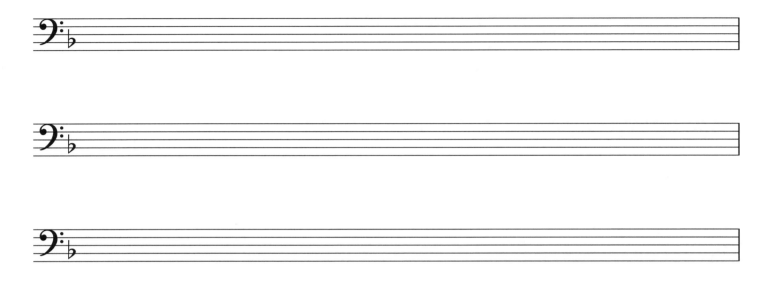

LISTEN 10 PLAY

Create a 2-chorus solo using any techniques you have learned. Memorize your solo, and practice it along with the recording.

LESSON 8
READING

CELLO PART

This *chart* (written part) uses symbols and instructions that direct you to skip around the pages. When you get the hang of these symbols, you will see that they help reduce the number of written measures, and make the chart easier to read quickly, at a glance. Sometimes, these directions are called the chart's *road map*.

2 BEATS DRUMS   Pickup. Short introduction (less than a measure).

[𝄋]   Sign. Later, there will be a direction (D.S., or "from the sign") telling you to jump to this symbol from another location in the music.

[⊕]   Coda symbol. "Coda" is another word for "ending." On the last chorus, skip from the first coda symbol to the second coda symbol (at the end of the piece). This symbol may also have the words "To Coda," or other directions (such as "last time only"). Often, you will just see the coda symbol by itself.

D.S. AL [⊕]   From the sign ([𝄋]), and take the coda. Jump back to the sign (first measure, after the pickup), and play from there. When you reach the first coda symbol, skip ahead to the next coda symbol (at the end).

AFTER SOLOS   When all solo choruses are finished, follow this direction.

[𝐁]   Different choruses may be marked with different letters. In this tune, the head is marked "A," and the improvisation choruses are marked "B."

SOLO   Solo chorus. Play this part when other musicians in the band improvise. When you play this tune with your own band, you might repeat this section several times, depending on how many people solo. When you solo, then obviously, you won't play this written part.

Play "Do It Now" along with the recording, and follow the written cello part exactly. Even if you have it memorized already, follow the part as you play.

Do It Now
Cello Part

By Matt Marvuglio

8 SOLOS

LEAD SHEET

Now play "Do It Now" with the recording, and work from the lead sheet. Create a solo, arco or pizzicato, and create your own bass part.

Do It Now

By Matt Marvuglio

CHAPTER II
DAILY PRACTICE ROUTINE

BLUES SCALE PRACTICE

Cello Register: High Notes/Low Notes

Playing in different registers will give you new tone qualities and sounds. A phrase played in the low register has a certain energy and intensity. The same phrase played an octave higher will have a different feel and sound.

Practice this register exercise, and when you are ready, practice it along with the recording. Notice the different characters between the registers.

CELLO PLAYERS AND CHORDS

Guitar and keyboard players often play *chords*—three or more notes sounded simultaneously. The cello can play chords, but more often, it will play the notes one after another, or as *arpeggios*.

"Do It Now" uses three different *dominant seventh* chords in its chord progression. Play them on your cello.

Chord tones (the notes of a chord) are important resources for notes when you improvise, similar to scales. Practice playing the chord tones for the chords in "Do It Now," using rhythms that fit the song's feel. Remember to swing your eighth notes. When you are ready, play this exercise along with the recording.

LISTEN **10** PLAY

SEVENTH CHORD EXERCISE 2

These exercises will help you develop your skills playing dominant seventh chords. It is in *descending form*— moving from high to low. Swing your eighth notes. Practice each chorus until you can play it easily, and then practice it with the recording.

LISTEN **10** PLAY

The second exercise presents dominant seventh chords in *ascending form*—moving from low to high.

LISTEN 10 PLAY

SOLO PRACTICE

Practice the first chorus of the solo to "Do It Now" along with the recording, reading the noteheads below. Use your ear to find the right rhythms.

LISTEN 8 PLAY

When you can play this solo, play the full tune without looking at the music—first the melody, then the solo (play the above chorus twice), and then the melody again to end it. Follow your ear, and try to match the violin on the recording.

> **PERFORMANCE TIP**
>
> If you make a mistake or get lost, keep your composure, and pretend that everything is going fine. Listen to the other instruments, hear what chords they are playing, and find your way back into the form. You can even practice getting lost and then finding your place. Start the recording at a random point within the track, and then follow your ear.

MEMORIZE

Create your own solo using any techniques you have learned. Memorize your part, and then play through the tune with the recording as if you were performing it live. Keep your place in the form, and don't stop, whatever happens.

SUMMARY

FORM	ARRANGEMENT	HARMONY	SCALE
12-BAR BLUES	PICKUP: 2 BEATS DRUMS	F7 Bb7 C7	F BLUES
(1 CHORUS = 12 BARS)	2 CHORUS MELODY		
	2 CHORUS SOLO		
	1 CHORUS MELODY		
	END: 4 M.		

PLAY "DO IT NOW" WITH YOUR OWN BAND!

"I Just Wanna Be With You" is a *blues swing*. *Swing* is a dance-oriented, big-band style from the 1930s. To hear more swing, listen to artists such as Count Basie, Benny Goodman, the Squirrel Nut Zippers, Diana Krall, Branford Marsalis, Kevin Eubanks, Joanne Brackeen, Cherry Poppin' Daddies, and Big Bad Voodoo Daddy.

LESSON 9
TECHNIQUE/THEORY

Listen to "I Just Wanna Be With You," and then play it along with the recording. This tune is a minor blues, similar to "Do It Now." The cello is doubled by the sax and guitar. Look for similarities between the three lines.

LISTEN **14** PLAY

PICKUPS

Each phrase of "I Just Wanna Be With You" begins on a weak beat (an eighth note before beat 4), leading to a strong beat (beat 1). Notes leading to a strong beat are called *pickups*. While you are preparing to play, count beats along with the rhythm section. This will help you come in at the right time.

Feel the pulse and count out loud. You come in after the third beat.

ARTICULATION: ACCENTS

Notes marked with accent (>) articulations are played louder than the rest so that they stand out. They are often the highest notes in the phrase.

Accents can make a phrase sound more spirited and energize a performance. Use them sparingly. If every note is accented, then nothing will stand out.

Practice accents along with the recording. Make accented notes stand out from the unaccented notes.

Accenting some of the notes in "I Just Wanna Be With You" will make the melody come alive—especially accenting notes that are unexpected, on beats that would ordinarily be weak, such as any eighth note off a beat, or beat 4. Practice it along with the recording. Make your accented notes stand out from the others.

WALKING BASS LINES

Listen to "I Just Wanna Be With You," and play along with the recording. Try to match the bass part. The bass line to this tune has three parts:

Notice that the three parts are similar. Hook up with the groove.

The bass line to this tune uses steady quarter notes, and it has a swing feel. This type of bass line is called a *walking bass*.

Walking bass lines connect chords. The root of the chord you are walking towards is called a *target note*. The bass line *walks* from one target note to the next.

When you create a walking bass line, first review the lead sheet or chord chart and locate the chord changes. These are your targets. Here is a chart for "I Just Wanna Be With You" showing its target notes:

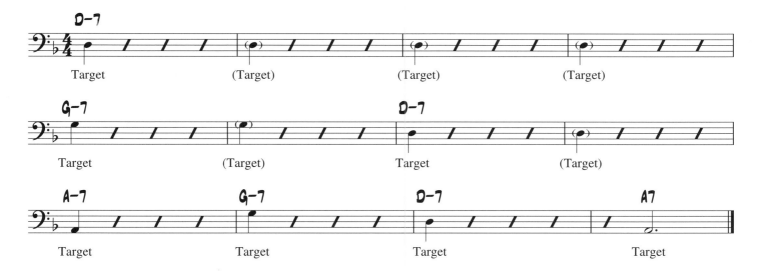

Chord roots are often played on the first beat of every measure, even when the measure doesn't have a new chord. The walking bass line approaches its targets using notes from scales, passing tones, and chord tones.

APPROACHING A NEW CHORD

The note before a target note is called an *approach note*. The recorded walking bass plays approach notes when going from one **D–7** chord to another:

Same chords:

D–7   (D–7)   (D–7)

Approach   Target   Approach   Target

In this tune, when the bass line approaches a new chord, the lick changes. When the bass line walks from **D–7** to **G–7** (below, measure 2 to 3), the C♯ approach note is replaced with a D, which is a chord tone (it is the root of the **D–7** chord and also the fifth of the **G–7** chord). This change in the lick, using a chord-tone approach rather than a non-chord tone approach, makes moving to the new target more smooth:

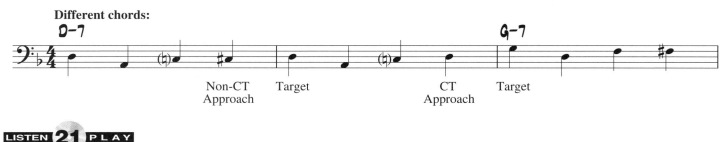

Different chords:

D–7   G–7

Non-CT   Target   CT   Target
Approach   Approach

LISTEN **21** PLAY

Listen to "I Just Wanna Be With You" and focus on the bass line. Notice how the walking riff changes when approaching new targets.

SKIPS

Though walking bass lines mostly use steady quarter notes, you can also include notes that hook up with the triplet feel. A common place for this is the last triplet note of a measure's last beat. This is called a *skip*.

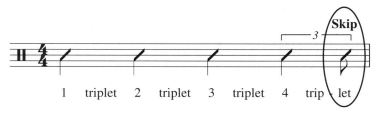

1 triplet 2 triplet 3 triplet 4 trip let

Play along with the track again placing a skip on every fourth beat. Play your skip at exactly the same time as they are hit by the hi-hat or other cymbals.

In this example, every measure has a skip. When you create your own bass lines, you can use them less regularly—every other measure, once per phrase, at the end of the form, or whenever you think they will sound good. You can play them on other beats besides the last one—beat 2 is a good choice too. You can repeat the note, play a different note from the chord or scale, or even just slap the string. Rhythm is the most important element here, not the pitches.

Play the recorded line along with the recording, but skip on the last beat.

Using skips and an accented backbeat will really make your walking bass lines swing.

PRACTICE TIP

Dance with your cello. Look at yourself in the mirror, as you play. Watch good dancers, when you are playing live. They'll get you in the right mood.

LESSON 10
LEARNING THE GROOVE

Listen to "I Just Wanna Be With You" and focus on the cymbals. This tune is a shuffle, like "Do It Now." There is a triplet feel under each beat. The main difference is that in this tune, the middle note in the triplet is left out. This is common in swing.

Shuffle
("Do It Now")

Swing Shuffle
("I Just Wanna...")

This syncopated "push-pull" feel is basic to jazz and r&b. Sometimes this feel is called a "double shuffle" because the drummer plays the same rhythm with both hands. In swing, the bass player usually plays a "walking" quarter-note bass line.

> ### PRACTICE TIP
>
> Record your practice, playing along with the CD. Then listen to your recording.
> How accurately and consistently are you playing?

HOOKING UP TO SWING

Listen to "I Just Wanna Be With You." Find the beat, tap your foot, and play along with the backbeat.

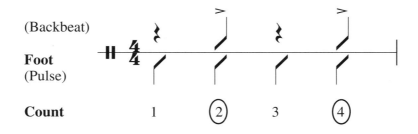

50

This tune has a swing feel, so count triplets on each beat as you play along with the backbeat. When you are ready, do this along with the recording. The circles show where to bow. The hi-hat matches your counting.

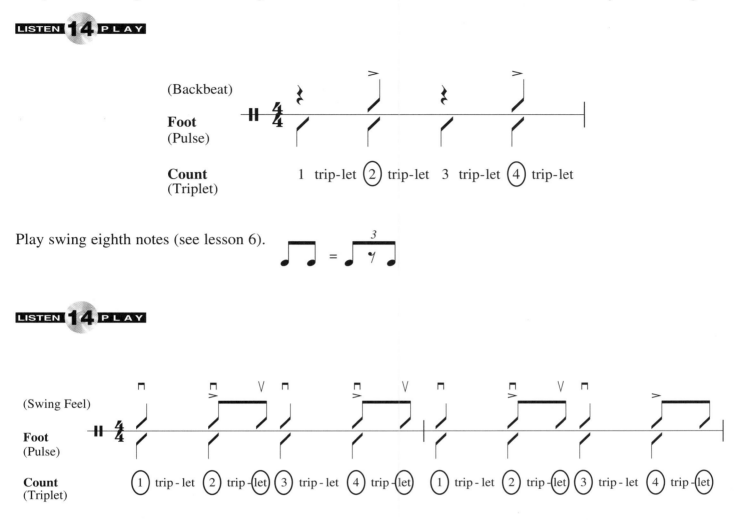

Play swing eighth notes (see lesson 6).

LEARNING "I JUST WANNA BE WITH YOU"

In this tune, the final note of the first measure is accented. Notes on the ordinarily weak beat 4 are usually not stressed, so this comes as a surprise—an interruption of the expected pulse. A rhythm such as this is called a *syncopation*. Syncopation is an important part of swing.

Bow the actual rhythms of the melody on your open D-string. When you are ready, bow along with the recording. Accent the notes that are marked.

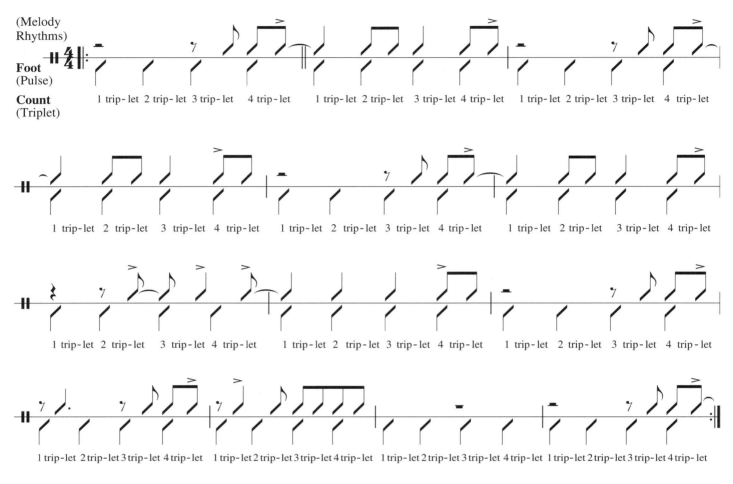

Play the actual part along with the recording. Tap your foot and count in your head, as you play. Use accents, and hook up with the groove.

LESSON 11
IMPROVISATION

FORM AND ARRANGEMENT

Listen to "I Just Wanna Be With You" and follow the form. This tune is another 12-bar blues. The form of each chorus is twelve measures long and divided into three phrases, just like "Do It Now." Is there an introduction or ending? What part of the form did these added sections come from?

LISTEN **14** PLAY

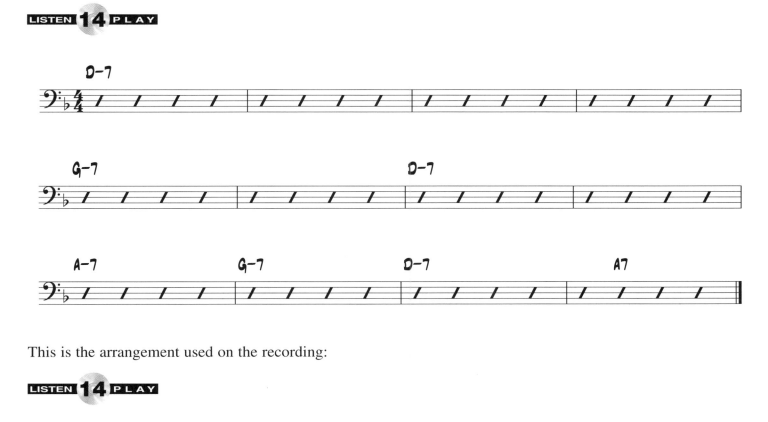

This is the arrangement used on the recording:

LISTEN **14** PLAY

INTRO	HEAD: 2x	CELLO SOLO: 2x	HEAD	ENDING
4 MEASURES	‖: 1 CHORUS = 12 MEASURES :‖	‖: 1 CHORUS = 12 MEASURES :‖	1 CHORUS = 12 MEASURES ‖	8 MEASURES

The intro and ending come from the form's last four measures. On the recording, the band chose to play the ending twice. This kind of repeated ending is called a *tag ending*.

PERFORMANCE TIP

Sometimes, a band may decide to "tag a tune" (play a tag ending) several times, building energy with each repetition. If things are going well and everyone is in the mood, a band may even make an ending longer than the rest of the tune. This is a place where people really let loose and have fun playing. When you listen to music, pay attention to what a band is doing at the end of a tune.

IDEAS FOR IMPROVISING

Scales: D Blues Scale

The D blues scale is a good one for this tune. Play it on your cello.

Practice the notes of the D blues scale over a wider range. Notice that it starts on an A. If you can, extend this range even higher.

D Blues Practice

LISTEN **15** P L A Y

Practice the D blues scale through this big melodic range, up and down, with the recording. Play each note in steady time, one per beat, and play as evenly as you can. Some notes, especially blue notes such as the A-flat, will jump out at you. Use these notes when you create your own solo.

When you're playing the melody, watch out for the rhythm in bar 6. Three notes in a row start on the "and" of the beats, not on the beats themselves. This syncopation is a very important rhythmic part of swing.

CALL AND RESPONSE

1. Echo each phrase, exactly as you hear it.

2. Improvise an answer to each phrase. Imitate the sound and rhythmic feel of the phrase you hear, and use the notes from the D blues scale.

LISTEN **16** P L A Y

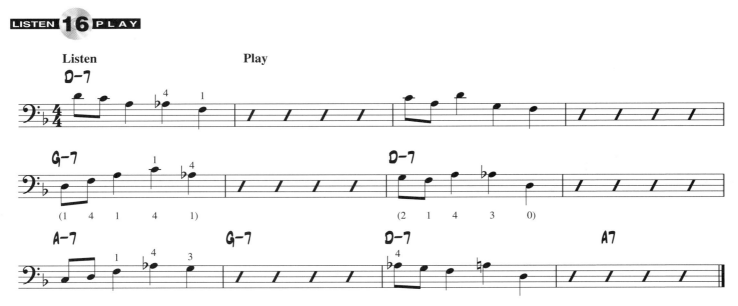

LISTEN **17** PLAY

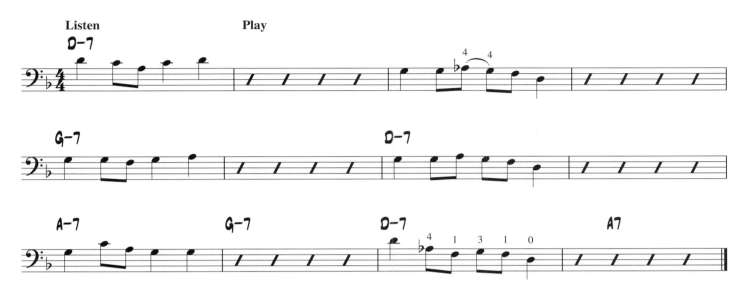

Listen   Play

Write out a few of your own ideas. Use the D blues scale.

LISTEN **15** PLAY

Create a 2-chorus solo using any techniques you have learned. Memorize your solo, and practice it along with the recording.

LESSON 12
READING

CELLO PART

Play "I Just Wanna Be With You" while reading from the written cello part. Play it as written.

LISTEN **15** P L A Y

I JUST WANNA BE WITH YOU
CELLO PART

BY MATT MARVUGLIO

A

LEAD SHEET

Play "I Just Wanna Be With You" from the lead sheet. Play the melody, improvise a solo, and create your own walking bass line.

INTRO/ENDING   Though this lead sheet doesn't show an introduction or ending, you and your band can create your own. The intro can be just drums, as you saw in "Do It Now," or it can come from the last line of the tune, as it does on the recording of this tune. Tag the ending at least three times, repeating the last four measures of the written part.

Since the melody is relatively short in length (twelve measures), you might want to play it twice when you are playing this tune with your own band. Play the pickups whenever you play the melody. You may or may not want to include them in your solo. If you are the only one in your band playing melody, try it up an octave, as written below.

I JUST WANNA BE WITH YOU

BY MATT MARVUGLIO

CHAPTER III
DAILY PRACTICE ROUTINE

ARTICULATIONS: CONSONANTS AND STACCATO (SWING STYLE)

Memorize the written melody, copying the phrasing and articulation of the cellist on the recording. How short or long are the notes? How do the notes begin? Imitate the sound and feel of the recorded melody as precisely as you can, and find ways to make your bow re-create the exact sound of each note.

When you are learning by ear, think about how each note begins. Notice that the notes on this tune often start with a hard sound, like P, T, or K. We call these note beginnings *consonant* sounds because they're the opposite of vowels, which are soft and fluid. Consonant sounds are harder and distinct. For consonant sounds, grab your string with the bow, and begin the note with a little "pop." This helps to define your notes rhythmically. Try to create this popping sound using different parts of your bow.

This sound is very common in swing, particularly on short, staccato notes. In swing, staccato is marked with a (^). To play this articulation, your bow should remain on the string and begin the note from a stop.

Practice swing staccato articulation along with the recording. In this exercise, the staccato markings help emphasize the backbeat. Be sure to start each note with a consonant articulation.

The recorded version of "I Just Wanna Be With You" uses a combination of staccato and accented notes. Articulating these notes differently energizes the whole melody line. Try to make each articulation stand out. Practice the articulations as shown, and then play it along with the recording.

CELLO SOUND

Imagining different "syllables," such as "tah," "tut," and "hut," will help you imagine different ways your bow can make a sound.

Practice long tones on your cello every day, and try to get as full and as warm a sound as you can. Here is an example of the kind of exercise you should do regularly. This one combines practicing long tones with practicing the D blues scale. Keep repeating this exercise for the whole track.

LISTEN **15** PLAY

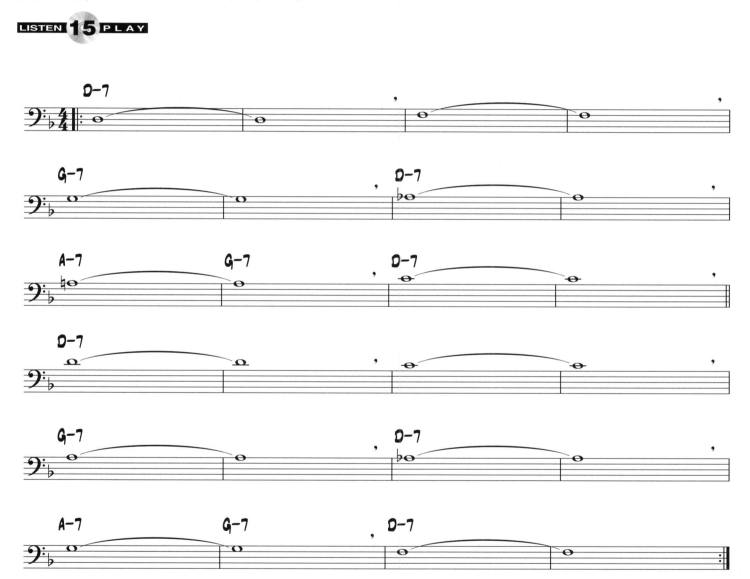

IMPROVISATION

Chords

The lead sheet to "I Just Wanna Be With You" includes four different chords. The first three are *minor seventh chords* and the last one **(A7)** is a *dominant seventh* chord. The improvised solo makes good use of chord tones.

Practice chord tones with the recording. Notice how different the dominant seventh chord (**A7** in the last measure) sounds—especially its note C-sharp. The different chord sound and the change in the groove make the last measure stand out and give the tune a unique character. It also helps the last measure to lead back to the first measure for when the form repeats. This is called a *turnaround* because it "turns the form around" back to the beginning.

LISTEN 15 PLAY

Improvising Using Chord Tones

LISTEN **15** PLAY

Practice this cello solo, and then play it along with the recording. Notice the use of chord tones.

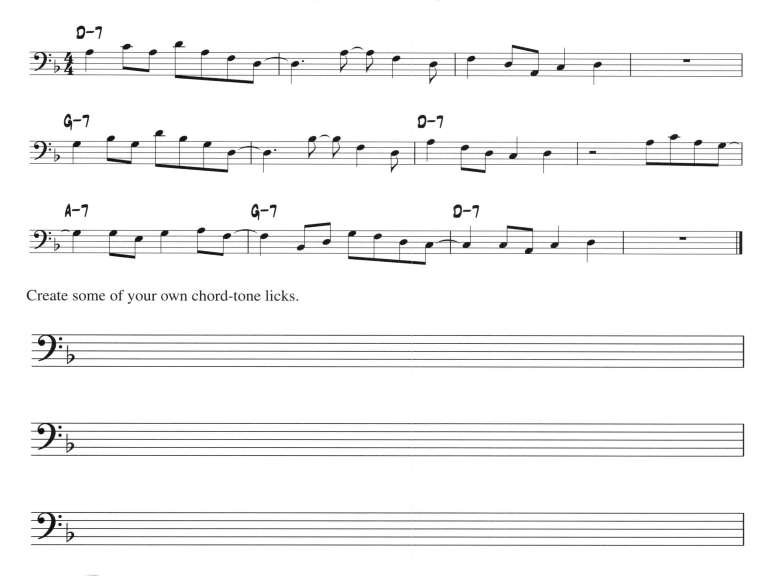

Create some of your own chord-tone licks.

LISTEN **15** PLAY

Create a 2-chorus solo using any techniques you have learned. Memorize your solo, and practice it along with the recording.

SOLO PRACTICE

LISTEN **15** PLAY

Practice the recorded cello solo to "I Just Wanna Be With You." When you are ready, play along with the recording.

MEMORIZE

Work on playing your own, personal interpretation of the melody of "I Just Wanna Be With You," with your own articulations and phrasing. Record yourself playing it along with the recording. Next, work on playing your own solos based on its chord progression, song form, and groove. Record your solos. Write down your favorite one and memorize it.

LISTEN **15** PLAY

SUMMARY

FORM	ARRANGEMENT	HARMONY	SCALE
12-BAR BLUES (1 CHORUS = 12 BARS)	INTRO: 4 M. 2 CHORUS MELODY 2 CHORUS SOLO 1 CHORUS MELODY END: 6 M.	D-7 G-7 A-7 A7	D BLUES

PLAY "I JUST WANNA BE WITH YOU" WITH YOUR OWN BAND!

"Leave Me Alone" is a *funk* tune. Funk has its roots in New Orleans street music. It started in the 1960s, and is a combination of rock, r&b, Motown, jazz, and blues. Funk has also influenced many rap artists. To hear more funk, listen to artists such as James Brown, Tower of Power, Kool and the Gang, the Meters, the Yellowjackets, Chaka Khan, Tina Turner, and the Red Hot Chili Peppers.

LESSON 13
TECHNIQUE/THEORY

Listen to "Leave Me Alone," and play along with the recording. Try to match the cello playing the melody.

LISTEN 18 PLAY

ARTICULATION: LEGATO

Notes marked with legato [–] articulations in jazz and pop styles are played for their full rhythmic value. Legato marks are similar to slurs, but the articulations are marked on individual notes, rather than whole phrases. When you are *sustaining* (holding) a legato note, counting eighth notes as you play will help you to be sure it lasts for its full duration—all the way up to the rest.

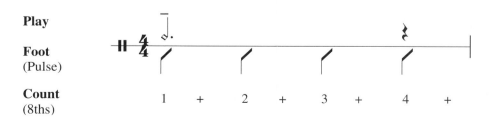

Practice playing notes legato along with the recording. Start and stop your notes as precisely as you can. Pay attention to the ends of notes as well as the beginnings.

Long, legato notes in a melody let listeners hear the rhythm section playing the groove. Short, staccato notes help the melody sound more like a part of the rhythm section. You can use a combination of both kinds of articulation.

Practice this articulation exercise with the recording.

BASS LINE

Chromatic Approaches

This bass line has *chromatic approaches* (half-step runs leading to a target note).

LESSON 14
LEARNING THE GROOVE

HOOKING UP TO FUNK

LISTEN **18** PLAY

Listen to "Leave Me Alone." This funk groove has its roots in New Orleans street music—funky march music played on marching instruments (snare drums, bass drums, and so on) still found in the Mardi Gras parades each spring. Many New Orleans artists were important to the development of funk.

Funk rhythms are played with less of a swing feel than blues. There is an underlying sixteenth-note feel, similar to rock, so count "1 e + a, 2 e + a, 3 e + a, 4 e + a," as you play. In funk, the backbeat (beats 2 and 4) is especially accented, usually by the snare drum.

This exercise will help you hook up to funk. Play along with the recording, and match the cello. The music is written out below. Find the beat, and play the melody. It emphasizes the strong, funk backbeat.

LISTEN **20** PLAY

SYNCOPATIONS AND ARTICULATIONS

How you articulate syncopations changes how they feel in the groove. In this next example, each lick is played legato and then staccato. Each one has a unique sound. Echo each lick exactly as you hear it, focusing on articulations. You may find that they are easier to hear than to read, so listen carefully, and try to copy what you hear.

LISTEN **21** PLAY

LESSON 15
IMPROVISATION

FORM AND ARRANGEMENT

Listen to "Leave Me Alone," and follow the form. This funk tune follows the 12-bar blues form.

LISTEN **18** PLAY

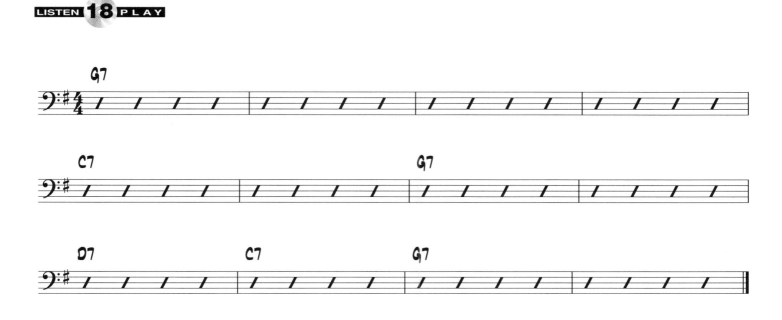

On the recording, the arrangement begins with a 4-measure introduction, featuring the rhythm section playing the groove.

INTRO	HEAD: 2x	SOLO: 2x	HEAD
4 MEASURES	‖: 1 CHORUS = 12 MEASURES	:‖: 1 CHORUS = 12 MEASURES	:‖: 1 CHORUS = 12 MEASURES :‖

IDEAS FOR IMPROVISING

Scales: G Blues

The G blues scale is a good choice for use with this tune. Play it on your cello.

Practice the notes of the G blues scale extended over a wider range. Start on low C, D♭, D, F, then up two octaves.

CHORDS

The chords to "Leave Me Alone" are all the same type: dominant seventh chords, which you saw in chapter 2. These chords have the same sound, with the same *intervals*—the distances between pitches. The only change is that they are *transposed*; they begin on different notes. When you improvise, favor the chord tones of the symbol shown above the staff. This is called "making the changes," or interpreting the song's chords in your own way.

Practice the chord tones to "Leave Me Alone." Below each tone is an interval number showing the note's relationship to the chord root. Since all chords in this tune are dominant seventh chords, the interval numbers are the same: root, 3, 5, ♭7.

RIFFS

Another good improvisation technique is to create a lick and then repeat it over and over. This repetition of a lick is called a *riff*. The lick's notes may come from a scale, from chord tones, from melody notes, or a combination of all three.

In the next exercise, we will play a riff built on this lick. Practice it until you can play it easily.

CALL AND RESPONSE

Echo each riff exactly as you hear it.

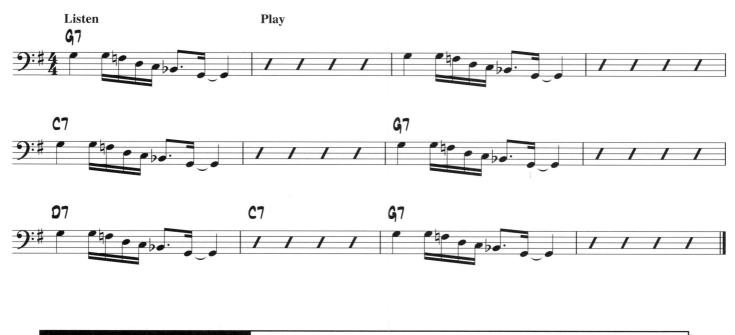

PERFORMANCE TIP

In blues, riffs work really well during a solo. They create musical tension, and the audience starts wondering how many times it will repeat before something new happens. The listeners move forward onto the edge of their seats, just waiting for a temporary conclusion—something that will relieve the musical tension and expectation that has been created.

WRITE YOUR OWN SINGLE RIFF SOLO

Create your own riff-based solo to "Leave Me Alone." Make sure the riff you create sounds good over all the chords. Write it out, and practice it along with the recording.

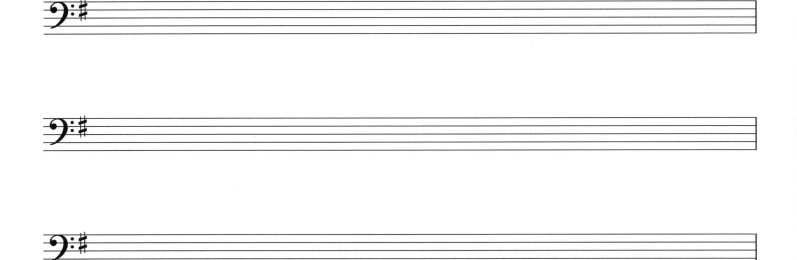

TRANSPOSING LICKS

To make a single lick sound good over several different chords, you have to keep it simple and only use a couple of pitches. If you want to use a more complex lick, you can transpose it to different notes, similar to how the dominant seventh chords earlier were transposed to begin on different roots.

Practice this lick a few times until you can play it easily. Since it is based on the tune's first chord (G7), you can think of it as being in the "original" key. Interval numbers are shown below each note.

To transpose this lick, move its root to the root of each new chord (C7 and D7), and then use the same intervals to find the other notes. Practice the lick based on all three chords until you can play them easily.

CALL AND RESPONSE

Echo each riff exactly as you hear it.

WRITE YOUR OWN TRANSPOSING RIFF SOLO

Create your own riff-based solo to "Leave Me Alone." Transpose the same riff over all the chords. Write it out, and practice it along with the recording.

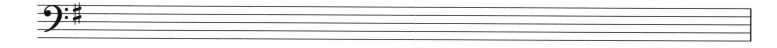

LESSON 16
READING

CELLO PART

CUE NOTES The small notes in measures 1 to 4 are *cue notes* showing the bass part. Read along with the bass notes to help you come in on time.

Play "Leave Me Alone" along with the recording, using the written cello part.

LEAVE ME ALONE
CELLO PART

By Matt Marvuglio

LEAD SHEET

Play "Leave Me Alone," and follow along with the lead sheet. Create your own riff-based solo. Try transposing the licks by ear, and play your own bass line.

LEAVE ME ALONE

By Matt Marvuglio

"Funky" ♩ = 82

CHAPTER IV
DAILY PRACTICE ROUTINE

VARYING THE RIFF

Funk riffs often have the root on the first beat, and often use the dominant seventh:

Root   Root   7

In this tune, the root and the dominant seventh begin every lick. The last three notes change each time:

Option 1

Option 2

Option 3

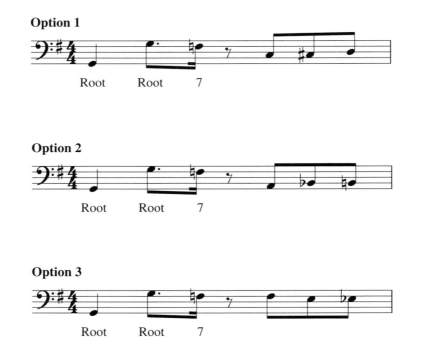

In the basic line and in option 1, the last three notes set up the root. In the other two licks, they lead to a new chord. Small changes to a given lick can make a solid, interesting bass line.

CHALLENGE

Create your own riff to "Leave Me Alone." Come up with a basic lick using the root and seventh, and then change it slightly in every measure. Accent beats 2 and 4, use some syncopation, and hook up with the sixteenth-note feel. Play your line along with the recording.

PERFORMANCE TIP

Keep your line simple. Funk bass lines should have a lot of empty space. Don't use too many notes. The root and the octave will keep your line grounded. Just a couple sixteenths in the bass line is enough to create a funk feel. Remember, the drummer will be playing sixteenth notes on every beat, so the bass doesn't need to do it all the time.

FUNK RHYTHMS

Practice this solo with the recording. Choose a combination of articulations to make your part groove with the rhythm section. Write your articulations into the score below.

LISTEN **19** PLAY

MAKING THE CHANGES

This solo draws its notes from three different sources. During **G7** measures, the notes come from the G blues scale. During the **C7** measures, the notes come from the chord tones of **C7**. During the **D7** measure, the notes come from chord tones of **D7**. Practice it alone first, and when you're ready, play it with the recording.

LISTEN **19** PLAY

PRACTICE TIP
The solo in the music above uses the same 1-measure rhythm over and over. If you learn that rhythm, the solo will become a lot easier to play.

SOLO PRACTICE

Practice the recorded cello solo to "Leave Me Alone." Before you play, read along with the recording, and finger the notes on cello without your bow. When you are ready, play along with the recording.

LISTEN 19 PLAY

MEMORIZE

Create your own solo using any of the techniques you have learned, and write it out. Practice it, memorize it, and then record yourself playing the whole tune along with the recording.

LISTEN **19** PLAY

SUMMARY

FORM	ARRANGEMENT	HARMONY	SCALE
12-BAR BLUES	INTRO: 4 M.		
(1 CHORUS = 12 BARS)	2 CHORUS MELODY		
	2 CHORUS SOLO	G7 C7 D7	G BLUES
	1 CHORUS MELODY		

PLAY "LEAVE ME ALONE" WITH YOUR OWN BAND!

"Affordable" is another funk tune, but it is lighter, with more of a feeling of open space. This style is popular with smooth-jazz artists. To hear more light funk, listen to artists such as David Sanborn, Earl Klugh, Walter Beasley, the Rippingtons, Dave Grusin, Kenny G, Bob James, and Anita Baker.

LESSON 17
TECHNIQUE/THEORY

Listen to "Affordable," and then play along with the recording. Try to match the cello in the melody.

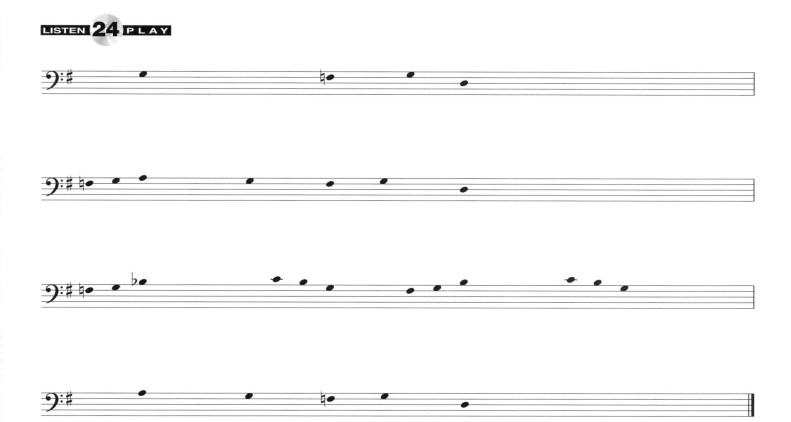

CHAPTER V

DYNAMICS

The melody of "Affordable" is made up mostly of long, drawn-out notes. The cellist on the recording makes this melody more interesting by changing the notes' *dynamics*—their loudness and softness. In this tune, the last notes of each phrase generally *decrescendo* (gradually become softer). The notation for decrescendos is a wedge (sometimes called a *hairpin*) opening to the left ($>$). This shows where the sound should be louder (above the lines' widest point) and where it should be softer (above where the lines meet). The opposite of a decrescendo is a *crescendo* (gradually growing louder), which opens to the right ($<$).

Practice the melody to "Affordable" with the recording, and decrescendo at the end of phrases 1, 2, and 4. Notice how dynamics help to shape the melody. If you can, try this up an octave.

LISTEN **24** PLAY

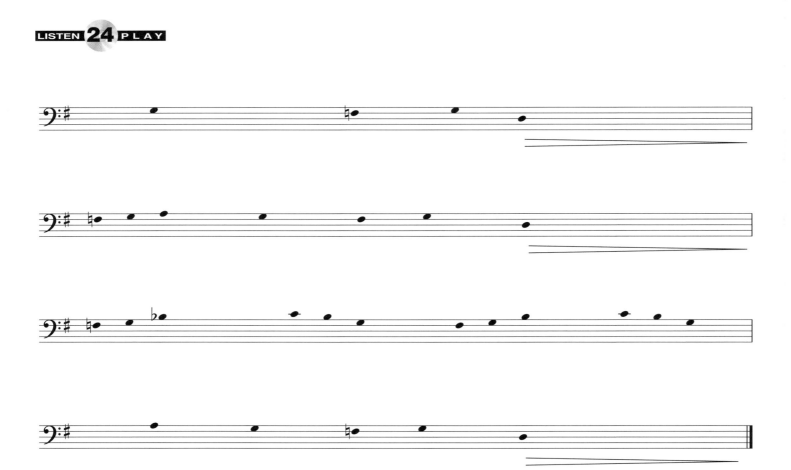

LESSON 18
LEARNING THE GROOVE

HOOKING UP TO LIGHT FUNK

LISTEN **24** PLAY

Listen to "Affordable." This groove is built around eighth notes, with some syncopated sixteenths in the B section. Notice that the band hooks up with the bass drum.

To learn this feel, practice counting sixteenths, leaving out the middle two sixteenths of each beat. Count out loud, along with a metronome or click track on the quarter-note pulse.

1 e + a   2 (e) (+) a   3 think think a   4   a   1   a   2   a   3   a   4   a

"Affordable" is a *light* funk tune. Like all funk music, eighth notes are played straight, not with a swing feel. The rhythm section plays fewer notes than they do in other styles of music. This makes the cello stand out even more than it does on the other tunes. The bass holds back more than it would with a *heavy* funk tune, such as "Leave Me Alone." To make it lighter, the bass part is quieter, and has fewer notes. What other elements of funk do you notice?

Listen to "Affordable." Find the pulse, and feel the sixteenth-note subdivisions. Notice that the backbeat is still emphasized, but it is lighter than it was in heavy funk.

CELLO IN THE RHYTHM SECTION

To hook up to a groove, try playing the rhythm section's parts along with the recording. This cello line combines the bass, guitar, and keyboard parts. Feel the backbeat and the sixteenth notes as you play.

There are two different grooves in this tune. Play this first riff during phrases 1, 2, and 4, and at the introduction.

LISTEN **25** PLAY

Play this riff during phrase 3.

LISTEN **26** PLAY

LESSON 19
IMPROVISATION

FORM AND ARRANGEMENT

Listen to "Affordable," and follow the 16-bar form.

LISTEN **24** PLAY

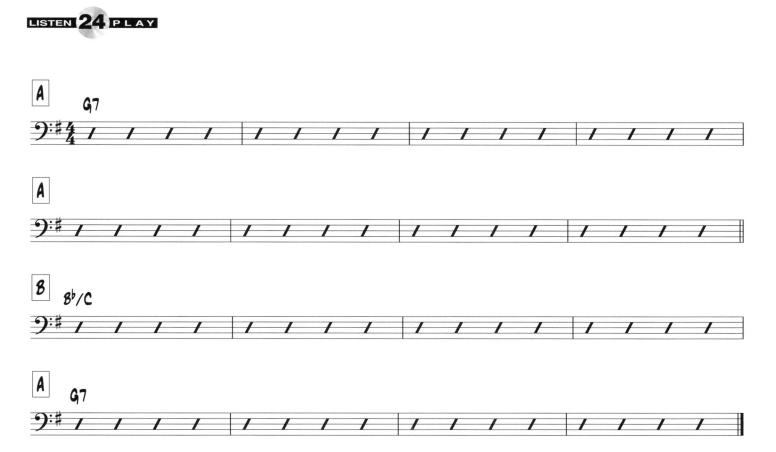

From practicing the rhythm section parts, you can tell that there are two primary musical ideas in this tune. When you play the melody, you can hear that there are two contrasting sections. Idea A is very sparse. It lasts for eight measures, with two phrases of cello melody. Idea B is in a more regular rhythm. It lasts for four measures. Then idea A returns for four measures. This form can be described as "AABA."

> **PRACTICE TIP**
>
> The 4-measure return of idea A at the end of the form may be confused with the eight measures of idea A that begin the new chorus. Altogether, there are twelve measures of this idea, so keep careful count.

Listen to the whole tune. Sing the melody while the cello plays the solo, and keep your place in the form. What is the arrangement on the recording? Is there an introduction or ending? Check your answer against the summary at the end of this chapter.

IDEAS FOR IMPROVISING

Scales: G Major and Minor Pentatonic Scales

The G major pentatonic scale will work well for improvising on this tune's A sections.

The G minor pentatonic scale will work well for improvising on this tune's B section.

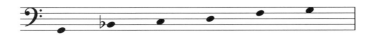

CALL AND RESPONSE

1. Echo each phrase, exactly as you hear it.
2. Improvise an answer to each phrase. Imitate the sound and rhythmic feel of the phase you hear, and use the notes from the G pentatonic scales.

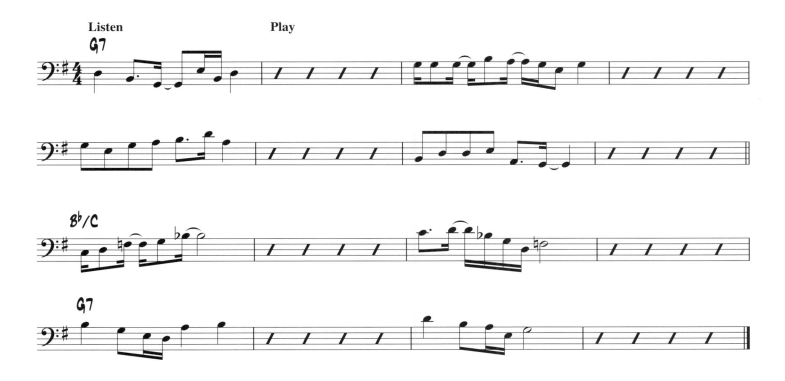

EMBELLISHING THE MELODY

The song melody is an excellent source of ideas for notes and licks. Whenever you play the melody, you contribute to the musical mood. The melody identifies the spirit and character of the song.

Think of the song melody as a compass. As you improvise, use it as your guide. Keep the melody at your solo's center, and improvise by adding or removing a few notes, or by varying their rhythm. Such changes are called *embellishments*.

Practice this embellished version of "Affordable." When you're ready, practice it along with the recording.

LISTEN **24** PLAY

Try playing the embellished version above "against" the original song melody. You can feel the added notes when you play them along with the original melody track.

Write out your own embellished version of the melody. Use the G pentatonic scales and the melody itself as sources for notes.

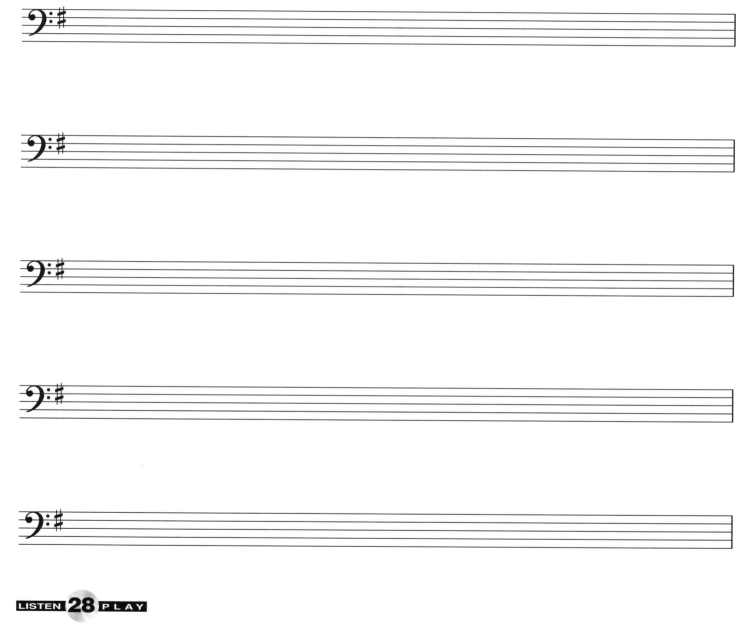

LISTEN **28** PLAY

Create a 1-chorus solo using any techniques you have learned. Memorize your solo, and practice it along with the recording.

LESSON 20
READING

CELLO PART

CELLO   Part label. The written parts you have been using were written specifically for cello. The key will also work for other instruments that read in C, or concert, such as keyboard or guitar. However, there may be some notation that will only make sense to a cellist.

Play "Affordable" while reading the cello part, and solo where indicated. This part includes cue notes showing the rhythm section (bass and keyboard) parts. Use these cue notes to help you keep your place.

AFFORDABLE
CELLO PART

BY MATT MARVUGLIO

LEAD SHEET

Play "Affordable" while reading the lead sheet. Play the melody, improvise, and make your own bass line.

AFFORDABLE

BY MATT MARVUGLIO

CHAPTER V
DAILY PRACTICE ROUTINE

VIBRATO

Another way to add interest to a melody (especially on notes of long duration) is to use *vibrato*. Vibrato is a slight, controlled vibration of a note's pitch, giving it a singing quality. In classical music, vibrato is used almost constantly. In the older popular styles, such as early jazz, vibrato is typically wide and rapid. In more contemporary popular styles, vibrato is generally used more sparingly, and with more variation in the speed and depth (variation of pitch) of vibrato. Many times, long notes begin straight, and then vibrato is added gradually. By listening to a lot of music, you will develop your own sense for when to use vibrato.

To add vibrato to a note, keep the center of your finger fixed on the fingerboard. Then roll your finger forward then back on the fingerboard around the center pitch, slightly raising and lowering the pitch. This is a technique where a teacher can be helpful. It is tricky.

Practice to get the most variety of speeds and depths out of your vibrato. That way, you'll have a wide palette of colors to use in your playing.

Practice long tones along with the recording. Start each note straight, then gradually add more and more vibrato to it, following the curvy line.

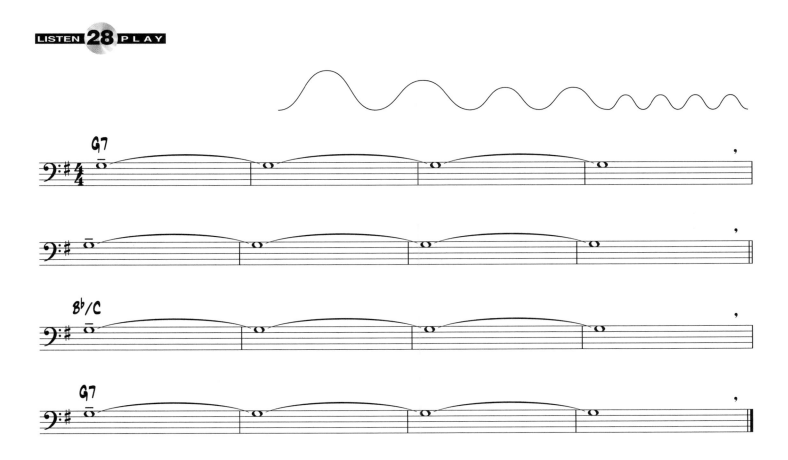

DYNAMICS AND VIBRATO

Try combining vibrato with dynamics, adding just a touch of vibrato at the end of phrases 1, 2, and 4. Don't overdo it! Just a little vibrato will sound great.

If you can play in second position (extended), follow the fingerings shown. Using them will avoid open strings and allow you to use vibrato on those notes.

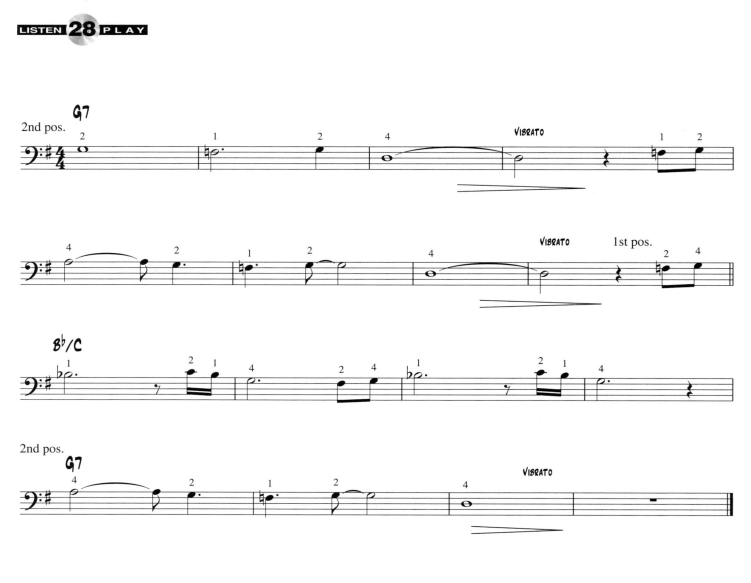

PENTATONIC SCALE PRACTICE

LISTEN **28** PLAY

Create a solo using the tune's chords and notes of the G pentatonic scales, shown below the cello staff. Try using different rhythms that hook up to the light funk groove. Practice your solo with the recording.

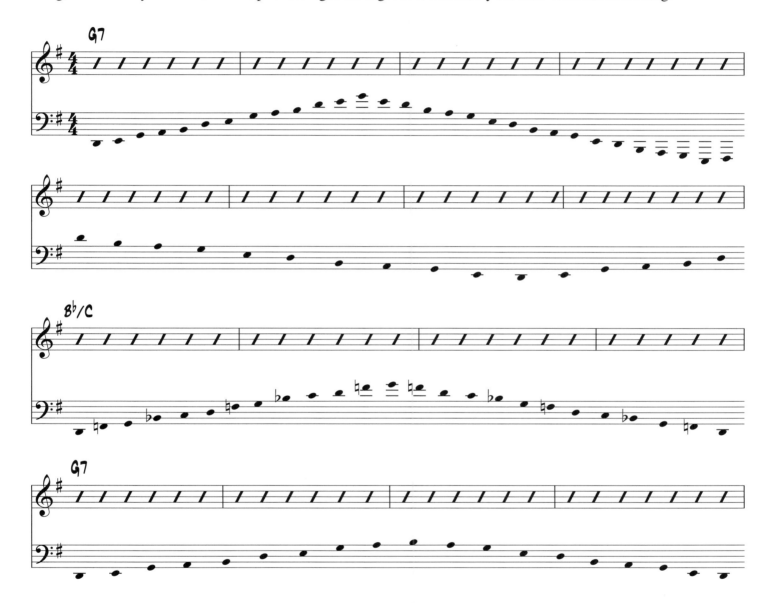

SOLO PRACTICE

Practice this solo along with the recording. Notice the use of the G pentatonic scales.

LISTEN **28** PLAY

MEMORIZE

Create your own solo using any of the techniques you have learned, and write it out. Practice it, memorize it, and then record yourself playing the whole tune along with the CD.

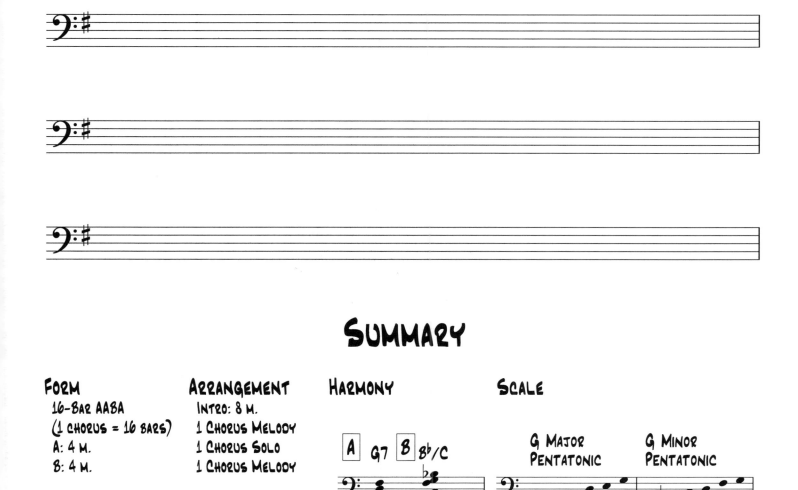

SUMMARY

FORM	ARRANGEMENT	HARMONY	SCALE
16-BAR AABA	INTRO: 8 M.		
(1 CHORUS = 16 BARS)	1 CHORUS MELODY		
A: 4 M.	1 CHORUS SOLO		G MAJOR PENTATONIC
B: 4 M.	1 CHORUS MELODY		G MINOR PENTATONIC

PLAY "AFFORDABLE" WITH YOUR OWN BAND!

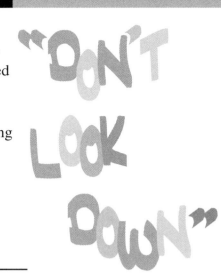

"Don't Look Down" is a *hard rock* tune. Hard rock first appeared in the late 1960s. It has characteristic heavy bass, long, drawn-out chords, and amplified instruments. To hear more hard rock, listen to artists such as Aerosmith, Metallica, Powerman 5000, the Allman Brothers Band, Rob Zombie, Godsmack, 311, Stone Temple Pilots, Black Crowes, Steve Vai, and Smashing Pumpkins.

LESSON 21
TECHNIQUE/THEORY

Listen to "Don't Look Down," and then play along with the recording. The cello and sax sometimes play in harmony, and the melody is doubled by the guitar. This tune has two different parts.

The first part has these four phrases.

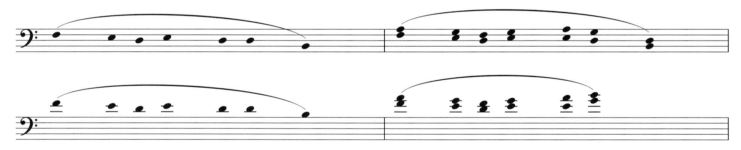

The second part has a riff that repeats four times.

It ends with the bass riff, played twice.

HARMONIZING A MELODY

If your band has two melodic instruments—a cello and a sax, for example—you might play the melody together and add some harmony.

The easiest way to add a harmony line is for one player to play thirds above or below the melody notes. This can be a little tricky, so follow your ear carefully. Some melody notes will sound better harmonized by a third above, some will sound better with a third below. If you are playing harmony, try to keep your harmony line smooth, and minimize the number of leaps you must take.

Notice the harmony lines in this tune. It lasts just a few notes and then returns to a unison melody. This is just one of many possibilities. How would you harmonize it? Try a few different ideas, and practice them along with the recording.

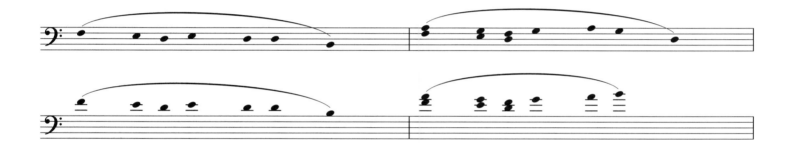

LESSON 22
LEARNING THE GROOVE

HOOKING UP TO HARD ROCK

Listen to "Don't Look Down." This tune has a standard rock/metal groove. It is a heavy feel, with very simple drum and bass parts. These parts must be simple because they are intended to be played in large arenas, where echoes would make busier parts sound muddy. It's a case of "less is more."

During the solos, the guitar doubles the bass, playing power chords in the second part. The keyboard plays sustained chords with an organ sound.

LISTEN 30 PLAY

Listen to the first part of "Don't Look Down." Chop along on the backbeats. Tap your foot on all four beats, and count out loud.

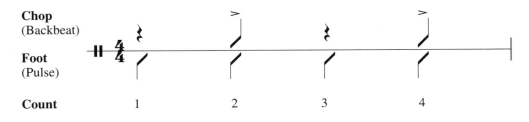

Try the same thing again. This time count the sixteenth notes out loud: 1e+a, 2e+a, 3e+a, 4e+a.

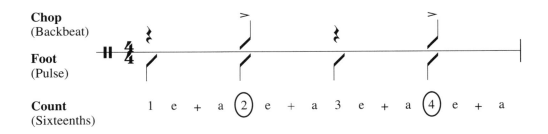

LEARNING "DON'T LOOK DOWN"

In the first part of this tune, the bass guitar plays a syncopated sixteenth-note riff. You hook up with that riff while you play the melody, and then you actually play the riff at the ending.

First, practice playing it on one note so that you can concentrate on the rhythm.

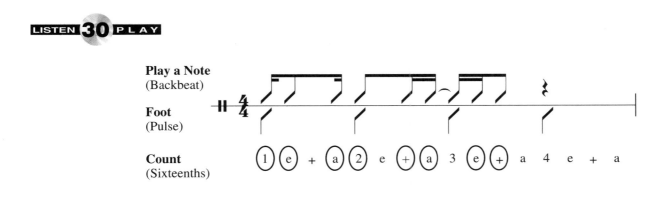

Next, play the actual notes. Hook up with the rhythm section. If you like, you can play this riff instead of the melody along with the A section of the full-band track.

The second part of this tune also has a syncopated sixteenth-note figure. Practice playing the rhythms to this lick (also used at the Intro).

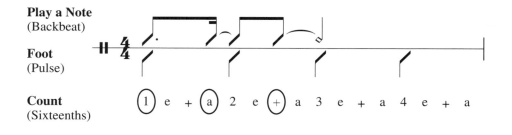

Play a Note
(Backbeat)

Foot
(Pulse)

Count
(Sixteenths)

① e + ⓐ 2 e ⊕ a 3 e + a 4 e + a

Practice the notes.

Practice the whole tune along with the recording, and hook up with the rhythm section.

LESSON 23
IMPROVISATION

FORM AND ARRANGEMENT

Listen to the recording and try to figure out the form and arrangement by ear. How long does each section of the form last? Is there an introduction or ending? For how many measures or beats does each chord last? Write down as much information as you can. Check your answers against the chord chart below and the summary at the end of this chapter.

LISTEN 29 PLAY

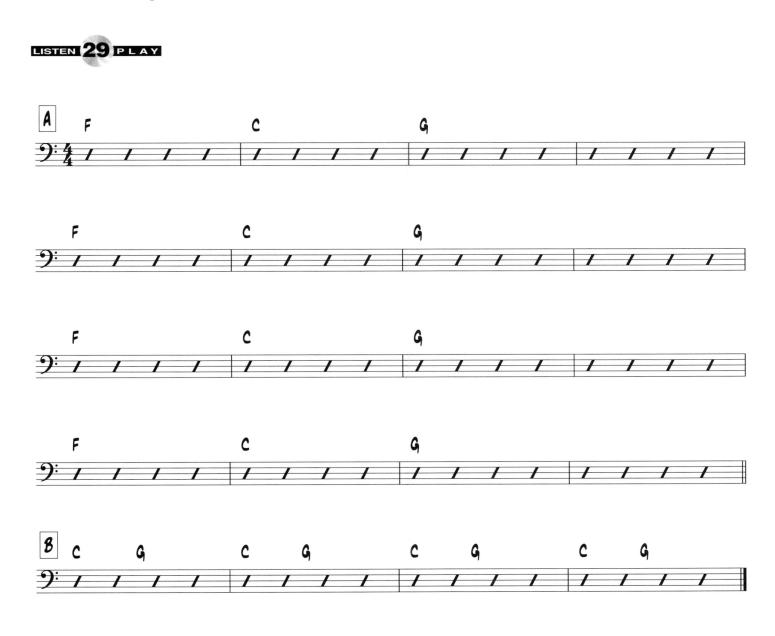

IDEAS FOR IMPROVISING

Scales: G Major and Minor Pentatonic Scales

The G major pentatonic scale will work well for improvising on this tune's A section.

The G minor pentatonic scale will work well for improvising on this tune's B section.

Practice both these scales. You can use both of them when you improvise, depending upon the chord.

CALL AND RESPONSE

Mixing Chord Tones and Pentatonic Scales

1. Echo the rhythm of each phrase exactly.
2. Improvise an answer to each phrase. Copy the rhythms of the recorded licks, but choose your own notes, based on the source indicated above the staff.

LISTEN **32** PLAY

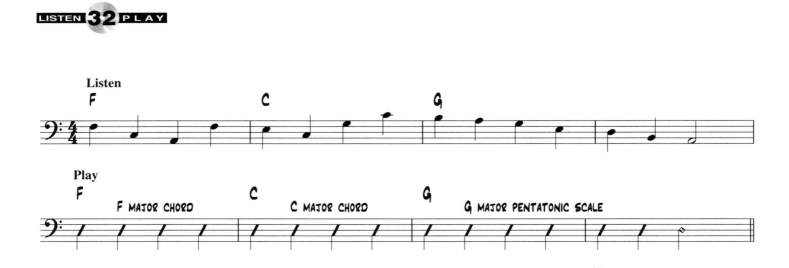

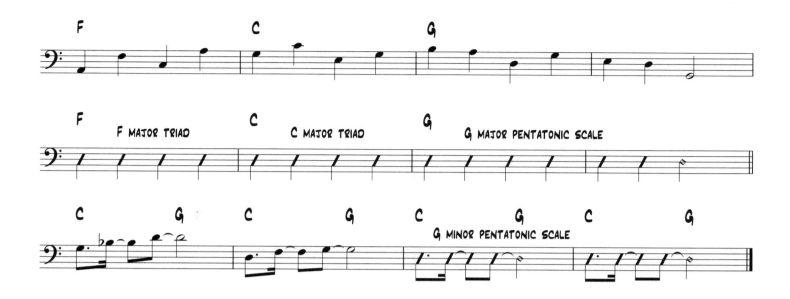

Write out a few of your own ideas.

Create a 1-chorus solo using any techniques you have learned. Memorize your solo, and practice it with the recording.

LESSON 24
READING

CELLO PART

1.   2.

:||

First and second ending markings. The first time you play these measures, play the *first ending*—the measures under the number 1. Then return to the begin-repeat sign (||:). The second time, skip the first ending and play the *second ending*—the measures under the number 2. Then, continue through the rest of the form.

Play "Don't Look Down" along with the recording. Use the written cello part.

LISTEN **33** PLAY

DON'T LOOK DOWN
CELLO PART

BY MATT MARVUGLIO

LEAD SHEET

Play your own part to "Don't Look Down," and follow along with the lead sheet.

DON'T LOOK DOWN

By Matt Marvuglio

CHAPTER VI
DAILY PRACTICE ROUTINE

EMBELLISHMENT PRACTICE

Practice embellishing the melody to "Don't Look Down." Play the written 4-bar embellished melody and then your own 4-bar embellished melody. Include the original melody notes, on their original beats, in your embellished melody.

PRACTICE TIP

There's an old saying: Good composers copy, and great composers steal. The best way to learn music is to listen, copy, and steal. Guitar players, singers, drummers—their sounds and playing styles should all be part of your treasure trove. Learn to improvise in the same way you learned language: listen, copy, create. Take a melody or an idea from somewhere, and embellish it. This is the way to become fluent and creative in your own musical language. Keep listening, copying, and stealing the music you like best, and then make it your own.

RHYTHM PRACTICE

This exercise will help you improve your ability to play steady sixteenth notes. Play any pitch or combination of pitches. Use a metronome, and start slow. Gradually increase the speed until you can play faster than the tempo on the recording (88 bpm). Then practice it along with the recording, using any pitch material we have studied. Simplify your pitches, if you need to. Focus on keeping steady time and articulating the accents.

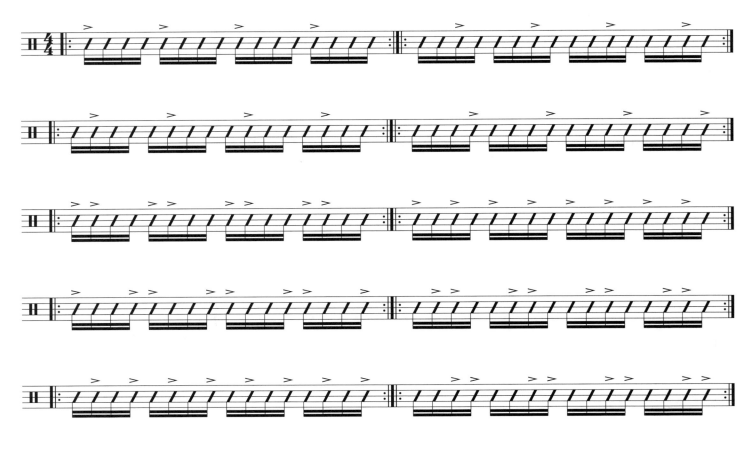

SYNCOPATION PRACTICE

Syncopated rhythms can be learned by expanding them into an easily readable form. The following examples illustrates this. In each line, the rhythm is exactly the same. It is just represented by different note lengths.

First Part

Second Part

INVERSIONS

Part of your technique is being able to play chords in different *inversions*. An inversion is an arrangement of chord tones. Practice these inversions for the "Don't Look Down" chords.

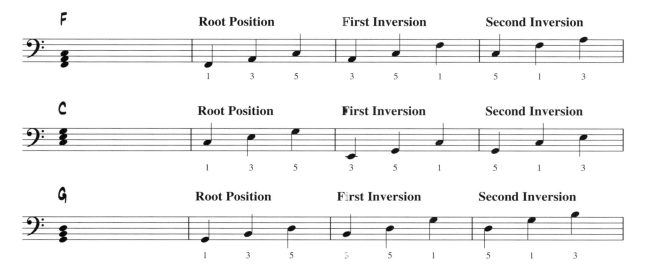

Inversion Practice

Practice this inversion exercise along with the recording. Become familiar with the sound of each chord and each inversion. Try using different inversions when creating bass lines for "Don't Look Down."

SOLO PRACTICE

Practice the recorded solo along with the CD.

MEMORIZE

Create your own solo using any of the techniques you have learned, and write it out. Practice it, memorize it, and then record yourself playing the whole tune along with the recording.

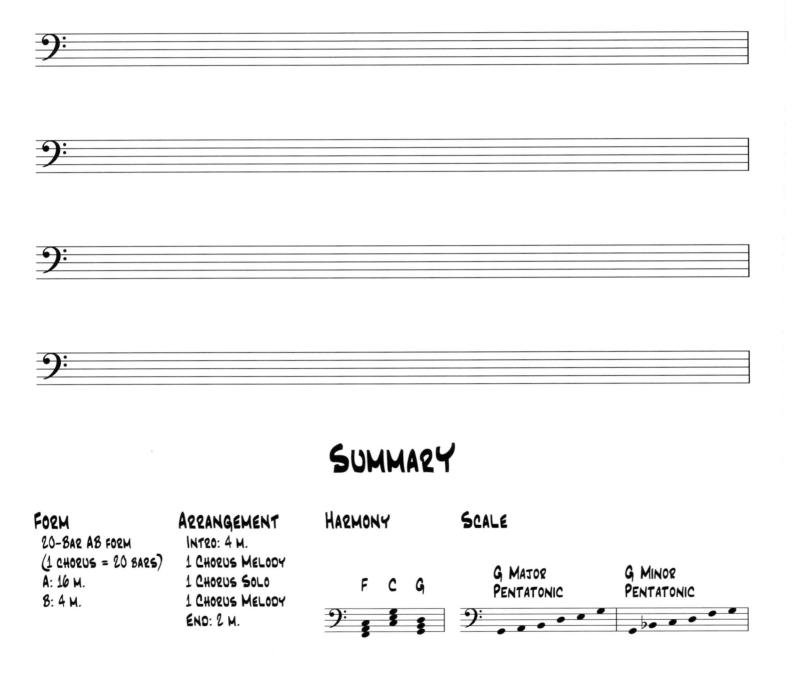

SUMMARY

FORM	ARRANGEMENT	HARMONY	SCALE
20-BAR AB FORM	INTRO: 4 M.		
(1 CHORUS = 20 BARS)	1 CHORUS MELODY		
A: 16 M.	1 CHORUS SOLO	F C G	G MAJOR PENTATONIC
B: 4 M.	1 CHORUS MELODY		G MINOR PENTATONIC
	END: 2 M.		

PLAY "DON'T LOOK DOWN" WITH YOUR OWN BAND!

"Take Your Time" is a *bossa nova* tune. Bossa nova began in Brazil, combining American jazz and an Afro-Brazilian form of dance music called *samba*. To hear more bossa nova, listen to Stan Getz, Antonio Carlos Jobim, Eliane Elias, Astrud Gilberto, Flora Purim, Dave Valentine, and Spyro Gyra.

CHAPTER VII

LESSON 25
TECHNIQUE/THEORY

Listen to "Take Your Time" on the recording. The melody is in two long phrases. Practice it along with the recording, and try to match the cello.

This is the first phrase.

This is the second phrase.

CHANGING KEYS WITHIN A POSITION

Within a position, the placement of your fingers will often change depending on the key or mode you are playing. The melody to "Take Your Time" is a good example of this.

In the following exercise, notice how your fingerings change, even though the home note (tonic) is always D. Practicing different scales within a position helps you to play in tune and develop muscle memory for different chords.

Practice it along with the recording. Then play "Take Your Time" again, and feel how comfortable it is to make these different finger placements.

LISTEN **35** PLAY

LESSON 26
LEARNING THE GROOVE

HOOKING UP TO BOSSA NOVA

Listen to "Take Your Time." This tune is a bossa nova, a style of music that originated in Brazil. Throughout the tune, a 2-bar rhythmic pattern repeats. This repeating pattern is an essential part of bossa nova. The drum plays it on a rim click.

LISTEN 34 PLAY

Repeating rhythmic structures are at the heart of much African-based music, including Afro-Caribbean and most South and Latin American styles.

The tune begins with a drum solo that sets up the bossa nova groove. Then the bass joins in, hooking up with the syncopated rimshot, as well as the bass drum. Bossa nova (sometimes just called *bossa*) has a straight eighth-note feel.

Bossa bass lines can be very simple. You can just play half notes, and it will sound fine. Play this half-note bass line with the recording, and count out eighth notes.

Here is a variation, with slightly more motion, using quarter notes:

Rhythm is what makes bossa nova unique—especially the "+" of beat 2. The drum beat will always play this critical syncopation, and the bass and other instruments can hook up with it too. Play this simple syncopated bossa nova bass line:

These examples all use single-measure licks. However, you can also have licks that last for two measures. You can change every other measure, and make the whole line more interesting. Dropping the octave is a common variation.

Play the written lick with the recording again, and notice its syncopated second beat. Also notice that the line uses only chord roots, fifths, and octaves.

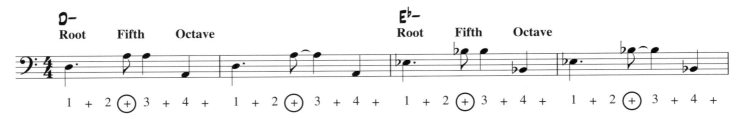

Play the snare drum rhythms, which sound the bossa nova pattern you saw at the beginning of this lesson. Hook up with the bossa nova groove.

LISTEN 35 PLAY

Play the keyboard's own 2-bar rhythm. You will be playing the top note of each keyboard chord. Match the keyboard on the recording. You may prefer to play this up an octave.

LISTEN 35 PLAY

CHALLENGE

Try to figure out the guitar part by ear.

LESSON 27
IMPROVISATION

FORM AND ARRANGEMENT

Listen to "Take Your Time," and try to figure out the form by ear. Check your answers with the chord chart and summary. Then continue with this chapter.

LISTEN **34** PLAY

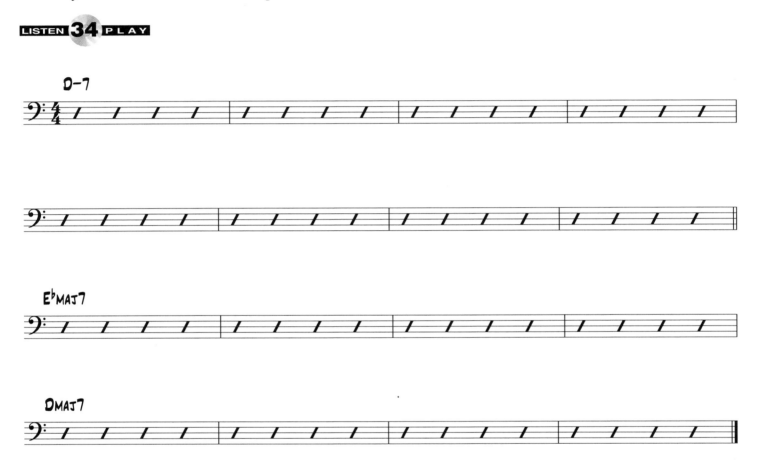

IDEAS FOR IMPROVISING

Scales: D Pentatonic Scales

For the first twelve measures of this tune (over the **D–7** and **E♭MA↓7** chords), we will use the D minor pentatonic scale to improvise. Practice this scale on your cello.

Practice the D minor pentatonic scale throughout your entire range.

In the last four measures (over the **DMA↓7** chord), solo using notes from the D major pentatonic scale. Major pentatonic scales work well when improvising on major or major seventh chords. Practice this scale on your violin.

Practice the D major pentatonic scale throughout your entire range.

BOSSA NOVA BASS LINES

Bossa nova bass lines usually have two notes: the root and fifth. You can also play octaves. Always play the chord root on the first beat of every measure. Bossa bass lines tend to be simple, with notes often held for more than just one beat.

CALL AND RESPONSE

1. Echo each phrase, exactly as you hear it.
2. Improvise an answer to each phrase. Imitate the sound and rhythmic feel of the phrase you hear, and use the notes from the D pentatonic scales.

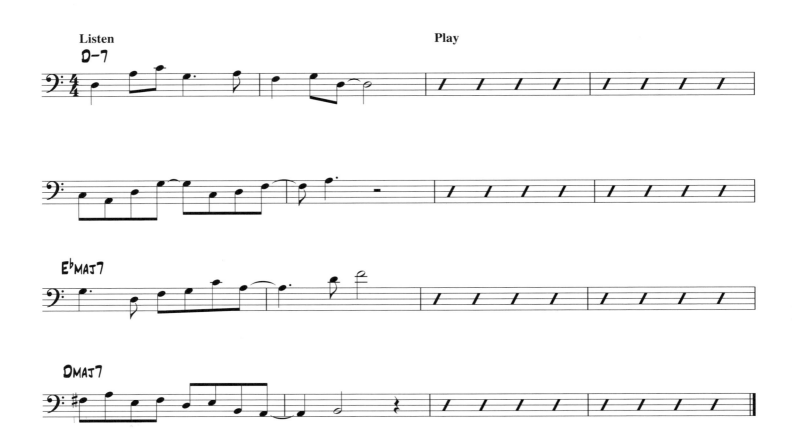

Write out some of your own ideas. Use notes from the D pentatonic scales.

LISTEN 35 PLAY

Create a 1-chorus solo using any techniques you have learned. Memorize your solo, practice it along with the recording, and then record it.

LESSON 28
READING

CELLO PART

$\frac{2}{\text{///}}$ Two-measure repeat. Repeat the previously notated two measures.

Play "Take Your Time," and use the written part. Alternatively, you could play the bass line or the keyboard line. Use the full band track (track 35), if you do.

LISTEN **35** PLAY

TAKE YOUR TIME
CELLO PART

BY MATT MARVUGLIO

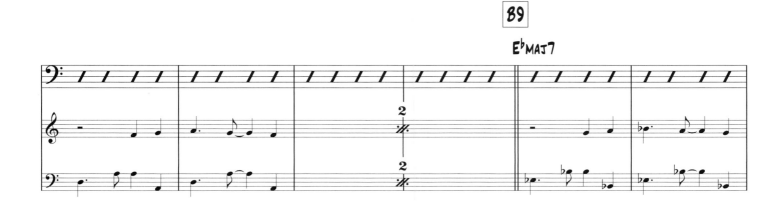

LEAD SHEET

Play "Take Your Time," and follow the lead sheet.

TAKE YOUR TIME

By Matt Marvuglio

CHAPTER VII
DAILY PRACTICE ROUTINE

CHORD TONES AND TENSIONS

A *tension* note is an extension of a chord. The example below shows extended chord arpeggios. They are another good source of notes to use in your solos. Tensions are marked with a T below.

Call and Response

1. Echo each phrase, exactly as you hear it. Notice the use of tensions.
2. Improvise an answer to each phrase. Imitate the sound and rhythmic feel of the phrase you hear, and use chord tones. Try using the same tension notes as you hear on the recording.

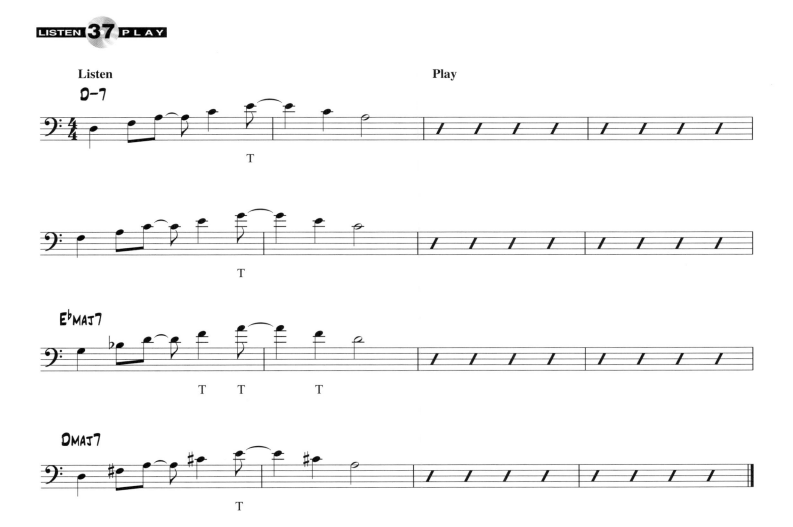

Write out some of your own ideas. Use notes from the D pentatonic scales and from the chord tones and tensions of D–7, E♭MAj7, and DMAj7.

LEARNING NEW SCALES

Chord tones and tensions are good sources for notes in your improvisations, as are scales. The pentatonic and the blues scales are great sources of ideas. There are many other scales that are also good sources of ideas. As you get comfortable with the chords and scales you know, you may wish to explore some new ones.

Learn to play any new scale using the same approach that you used to learn the simpler ones.

1. One octave. Play the scale in just one octave, up and down, so that you can focus on what the pitches are.
2. Full range. Practice it throughout the whole range of your cello, as low and as high as you can go.
3. Rhythmic and melodic figures. Practice it in rhythm, against a metronome or a recording, making up little melodic and rhythmic figures using the notes from the scale, similar to the exercises you've been doing in this book.
4. Write a solo. Write out a solo that uses the new scale(s).

Once you get a new scale under your fingers, you will be able to use it musically. Writing out some melodies based on your new sources of notes is a great way to help you master them. Try to use all these techniques with the following three scales that can be used with "Take Your Time."

The D Dorian scale (or "mode") will work well over the **D-7** chords of "Take Your Time."

The D Phrygian scale will work well over the **E♭MAJ7** chords.

The D major scale will work well over the **DMAJ7** chords.

Practice these scales using the above approach. Make sure to adjust your finger placement, as shown in lesson 25. When you go from the major scale to Dorian, use your second finger. And then when you go from there to Phrygian, extend your first finger down a half step.

As you practice new scales or other sources of ideas, concentrate on each note you play, listen carefully, and adjust your fingers to match your ear.

SOLO PRACTICE

Practice the recorded solo along with the recording. Notice the use of long tones, chord tones, and tensions.
What scales seem to be used?

MEMORIZE

Create your own solo using any of the techniques you have learned, and write it out. Practice it, memorize it, and then record yourself playing the whole tune along with the recording.

LISTEN **35** PLAY

SUMMARY

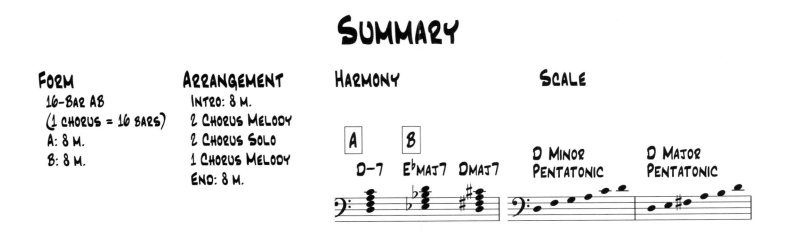

FORM
16-BAR AB
(1 CHORUS = 16 BARS)
A: 8 M.
B: 8 M.

ARRANGEMENT
INTRO: 8 M.
2 CHORUS MELODY
2 CHORUS SOLO
1 CHORUS MELODY
END: 8 M.

HARMONY

SCALE

PLAY "TAKE YOUR TIME" WITH YOUR OWN BAND!

"Stop It" is a blues/jazz tune in which *stop time* accents the melody, like a question and answer. Stop-time is very common in blues, jazz, and other styles. To hear more stop-time blues, listen to artists such as Miles Davis, John Coltrane, Jim Hall, Sarah Vaughn, Bill Evans, Ella Fitzgerald, Louis Armstrong, Abbie Lincoln, Dizzy Gillespie, and Charlie Parker.

CHAPTER VIII

LESSON 29
TECHNIQUE/THEORY

Listen to the recording and then play along with the melody. Try to match the cello. Notice that there are only three different licks.

LISTEN 38 PLAY

ARTICULATION

A way to make this melody come alive is by using different articulations for the licks. The first, third, and fifth lick should all be played legato, with the notes sounding connected to each other. This is often marked with a slur. Only the first note should be articulated.

The second lick (repeated after licks 3 and 5) is made up of five notes with alternating short accents (swing staccato) and legato articulations.

The lick at bar 9 is also legato.

Practice the melody along with the recording, articulating these licks as shown above.

LESSON 30
LEARNING THE GROOVE

HOOKING UP TO STOP-TIME BLUES

Listen to "Stop It." This jazz cymbal beat is at the heart of jazz rhythm. The "spang spang a-lang" cymbal beat is unique to jazz, and it has been its primary pattern since the 1940s. Its underlying pulse is the same as the shuffle. This pattern has accompanied Count Basie, Miles Davis, John Coltrane, Duke Ellington, and thousands of other jazz artists.

LISTEN **38** PLAY

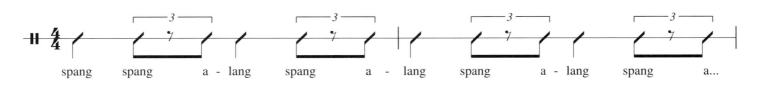

spang   spang   a - lang   spang   a - lang   spang   a - lang   spang   a...

STOP TIME

In stop time, the groove is punctuated by *stop-time kicks*. These are rhythmic figures, usually just one or two beats long, that punctuate the melody. That is why it is called "stop time"—the rhythm section "stops" or rests.

Play the melody along with the recording, and match the cello part. On this tune, the cello plays the melody during the stop-time sections. Tap the pulse with your foot, and feel the subdivisions. Hook up with the groove.

LISTEN **39** PLAY

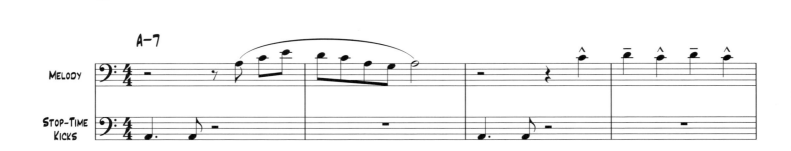

REGULAR TIME

During the solos, the rhythm section *plays time*. The drums play a steady beat, the bass *walks* (plays steady quarter notes), and the keyboard and guitar play chords.

The guitar plays chords in a 2-measure pattern. Play the guitar part (the top notes of its chords) along with the recording. Match the guitar's articulation and time feel. You might prefer to play this up an octave.

The keyboard also has a repeating 2-measure pattern. Play the keyboard part (the top notes of its chords) along with the recording. Match the keyboard's articulation and time feel, and notice how it hooks up with the guitar part. You might prefer to play this up an octave.

WALKING BASS: LINES THAT BREATHE

When you play swing, you want to create a danceable time feel. Your line should breathe. Here are a few things you can do to make your walking bass lines come alive.

1. Note length. Notes shouldn't be too short or too long, and they don't all have to be the same. Even though you are playing on every beat, the line and time needs to breathe, and have a sense of phrasing, or it will sound stiff.

> ### PRACTICE TIP
> The way you breathe affects the way you play. Pay attention to how you breathe when you play, and match your articulations to your breath. Practice breathing short breaths when you play short notes and long breaths when you play long notes.

2. Note weight. Varying the weight of each note will also help your bass line breathe. The root on the first beat is usually heavy.

   Roots are "heavier" than other chord tones. Try moving the root to beats other than the downbeat.

3. Range. Most walking lines are in the middle range of the instrument. Use high and low notes for variety. Similarly, chord tones are stable, and approach notes add variety.

LESSON 31
IMPROVISATION

FORM AND ARRANGEMENT

Listen to "Stop It," and try to figure out the form and arrangement by ear. Check your answer against the summary at the end of this chapter.

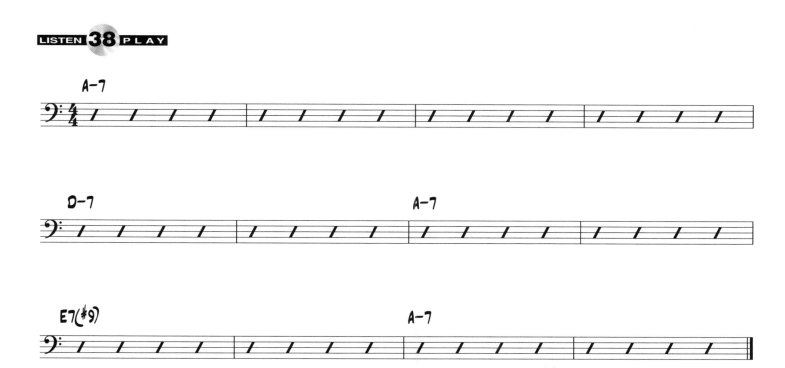

IDEAS FOR IMPROVISING

Scales: A Blues

Use the A blues scale to improvise over this tune.

Practice the notes of the A blues scale throughout the entire range of your cello.

Practice playing the chord tones used in this tune. Notice the extension of the **E7(♯9)** chord.

The **E7(♯9)** chord has a dissonance between the G-natural and the G-sharp. This color is one of the defining elements of the chord progression, and will lend a distinctive color to your solo. Here is an example of the kind of lick you can play that makes use of that dissonance.

CALL AND RESPONSE

1. Echo each phrase, exactly as you hear it.
2. Improvise an answer to each phrase. Imitate the sound and rhythmic feel of the phrase you hear. Use the A blues scale, chord tones, and tensions.

Write out some of your own ideas. Use chord tones and notes from the A blues scale.

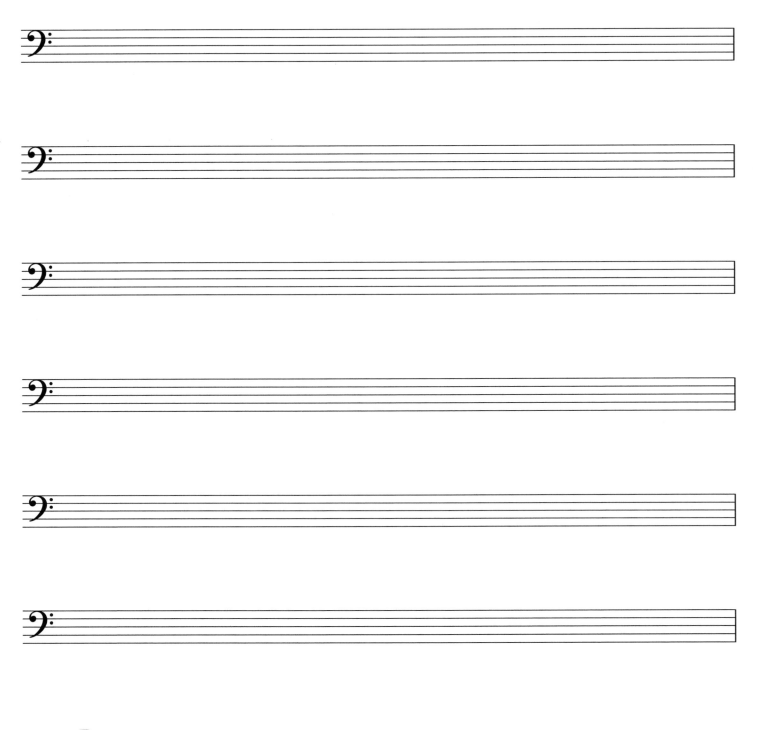

Create a 2-chorus solo using any techniques you have learned. Memorize your solo, and practice it along with the recording.

LESSON 32
READING

CELLO PART

D.C. AL ⊕   From the beginning, and take the coda. Jump to the very first measure of the tune, and play from there. When you reach the first coda symbol, skip ahead to the next coda symbol (at the end). This is similar to the "**D.S. AL CODA**," but instead of going to a sign, go to the first measure of the tune.

Play "Stop It" along with the recording, and read from the written cello part.

LISTEN **43** PLAY

STOP IT
CELLO PART

By Matt Marvuglio

LEAD SHEET

Play "Stop It" from the lead sheet.

STOP IT

BY MATT MARVUGLIO

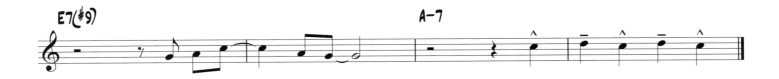

CHAPTER VIII
DAILY PRACTICE ROUTINE

SCALE PRACTICE

As you become comfortable with all the different scales and chords, you will find it easier to use them. Practice them every day as part of your routine. You will learn them thoroughly, and your general technique, facility, and stamina will also improve as a result.

Here are some more strategies for practicing scales.

1. **Practice scales in all twelve keys.** Begin with the key of a tune that you are working on. For "Stop It," we're in the key of A minor, so if you were practicing minor scales, you might begin by practicing the A minor scale. Then move the scale up a fifth (or down a fourth), and practice the E minor scale. Then the B minor scale. Keep moving the scale up a fifth (or down a fourth) until you are back at the key of A minor. This is called the "circle of fifths."

Continue…

Some scales are easier on the cello and some are more difficult. The keys of D and A are relatively easy, while the keys of D♭ and F♯ are relatively difficult. Practice slowly, and listen to make sure that you are in tune. With practice, you'll get used to all of them. The notes in all the major scales have the same relationships to each other, so as you get used to these relationships, generally, they will all become easier to play.

2. **Practice scales in thirds.** Play the scale, but skip every other note. For A minor, you'd play A, C, B, D, C, E, D, F.... When the range gets too high, drop back down to your lowest octave, and pick up where you left off. Try this in all twelve keys.

Continue…

3. **Practice scales in triads.** Starting from the tonic note, play a triad using only scale tones. Then play a triad from the second note. This will help show you what triads are a natural part of the scale, and all kinds of chords will begin to fall naturally under your fingers. (These are called *diatonically occurring triads.*) Try this in all twelve keys.

Continue…

4. **Practice scales in seventh chords.** This is like practicing scales in triads, but you play four notes in each series: A, C♯, E, G♯; B, D, F♯, A; C♯, E, G♯, B....

Continue…

5. **Try different variations.** Invent your own similar exercises, such as trying different permutations (variations, or different orders) of each of the above exercises, or from any other source. For example, a variation of scales in thirds would be to first play a scale going upward in thirds, but then play the next scale in the circle of fifths going downward in thirds, alternating directions each time.

A Minor   E Minor   B Minor

Continue…

Or start the exercises by playing thirds going downward.

A Minor   E Minor   B Minor

Continue…

6. Practice scales over tunes. Decide what scales you will use over each chord, and then practice soloing along with a recording, using the right scale exercise over the right chord. In this example, you can see how the A minor was used at the beginning of the solo, then it switches to D blues, and then to A blues.

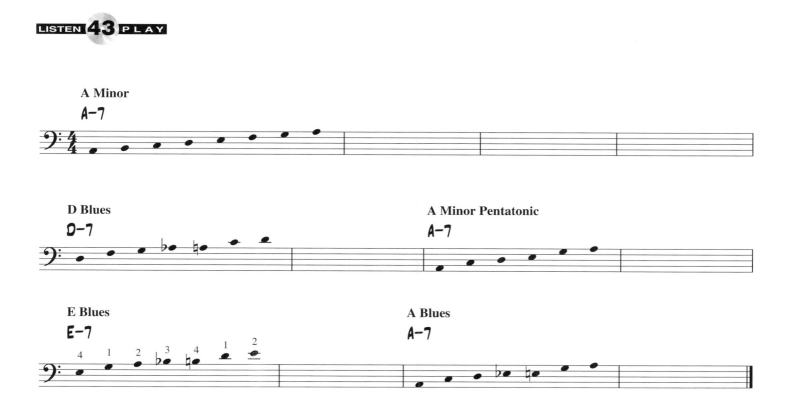

CHORD TONE PRACTICE

Practicing the chord tones of tunes is good for your technique because it involves big interval jumps and challenging string crossings. When practicing chord tones for technique, watch your bow carefully, and make sure you're only hitting one string at a time. Try to plan your fingering for more than one note at a time. That way, your fingers will get to a note before your bow does.

Practice this melody, which uses chord tones and tensions of the chords to "Stop It."

CALL AND RESPONSE

1. Echo each phrase, exactly as you hear it.
2. Improvise an answer to each phrase. Use the rhythms shown and choose notes from the chord tones shown below the staff. Be sure to mix up the chord tones, rather than playing them in the order shown.

Listen   Play

Write out a few of your own ideas. Use chord tones and the A blues scale.

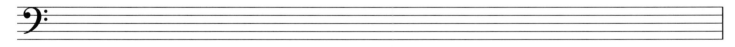

Create a 2-chorus solo using any techniques you have learned. Memorize your solo, and practice it along with the recording.

SOLO PRACTICE

Practice the recorded cello solo along with the CD.

LISTEN **43** PLAY

III. II.

MEMORIZE

Create your own solo using any of the techniques you have learned, and write it out. Practice it, memorize it, and then record yourself playing the whole tune along with the recording.

TECHNIQUE: INVERSIONS

Practice these inversions:

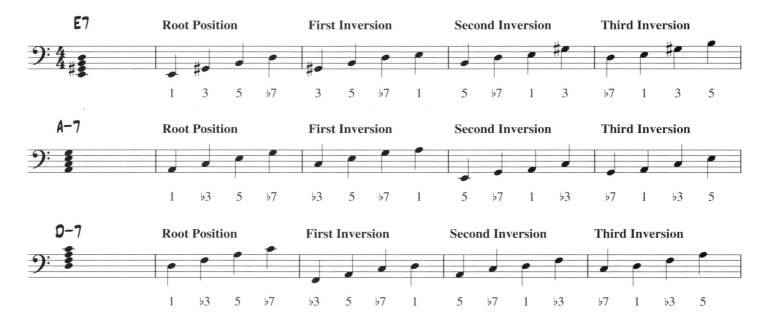

Inversions

This walking bass line uses many inversions. Practice it along with the recording.

SKIP PRACTICE

You have seen how skips can make a walking line more interesting. Skips can appear on any beat, not just the last beat. You can also play triplets on any beat. Open-string notes are good choices to use in these triplets, as they can be played quickly.

Practice this bass line, and then play it along with the recording. Practice it slowly at first. Notice the shape of the line.

CHALLENGE

Create your own bass line, using one triplet-feel figure—a skip or a triplet—in every measure.

SUMMARY

FORM	ARRANGEMENT	HARMONY	SCALE
12-BAR BLUES (1 CHORUS = 12 BARS)	2 CHORUS MELODY 4 CHORUS SOLO 2 CHORUS MELODY END: 1 M.	A-7 D-7 E7(♯9)	A BLUES

CHALLENGE

Create your own cello line, using one triplet-feel figure—a skip or a triplet—in every measure.

PLAY "STOP IT" WITH YOUR OWN BAND!

FINAL REMARKS

Congratulations on completing the *Berklee Practice Method*. You now have a good idea of the role of the cello in a band, and have command of the eight grooves/time feels of these tunes. The melodies and harmonic progressions that you have learned are important and useful parts of your musical vocabulary. In addition, you have tools and ideas for creating your own parts and solos. This is a great start!

What to do next? Play along with your favorite recordings. Find records that you hear other musicians talking about. Learn these tunes, grooves, and parts. There is a good reason that musicians talk about certain bands, albums, or cellists. Continue your theory, reading, and technique work. Investigate chord scales and modes. Learn all your key signatures (major and minor), scales, and chord arpeggios.

Develop your concept of what it means to play cello. Realize how important you are as a cellist in a band. You have a big responsibility, taking care of the melody, the harmony, and the groove. It is a powerful position.

Play your cello every day, by yourself and with others, and get the sound in your body.

Keep the beat!

—Matt and Mimi

More Fine Publications from Berklee Press

WOODWINDS

FAMOUS SAXOPHONE SOLOS
arr. Jeff Harrington
50449605 Book $14.99

IMPROVISATION FOR FLUTE
by Andy McGhee
50449810 Book $14.99

IMPROVISATION FOR SAXOPHONE
by Andy McGhee
50449860 Book $14.99

SAXOPHONE SOUND EFFECTS
by Ueli Dörig
50449628 Book/CD $14.99

ROOTS MUSIC

BEYOND BLUEGRASS
Beyond Bluegrass Banjo
by Dave Hollander and Matt Glaser
50449610 Book/CD $19.99
Beyond Bluegrass Mandolin
by John McGann and Matt Glaser
50449609 Book/CD $19.99
Bluegrass Fiddle and Beyond
by Matt Glaser
50449602 Book/CD $19.99

BERKLEE PRACTICE METHOD

GET YOUR BAND TOGETHER
With additional volumes for other instruments, plus a teacher's guide.
Bass
by Rich Appleman, John Repucci and the Berklee Faculty
50449427 Book/CD $14.95
Drum Set
by Ron Savage, Casey Scheuerell and the Berklee Faculty
50449429 Book/CD $14.95
Guitar
by Larry Baione and the Berklee Faculty
50449426 Book/CD $16.99
Keyboard
by Russell Hoffmann, Paul Schmeling and the Berklee Faculty
50449428 Book/CD $14.95

WELLNESS

MANAGE YOUR STRESS AND PAIN THROUGH MUSIC
by Dr. Suzanne B. Hanser and Dr. Susan E. Mandel
50449592 Book/CD $29.99

MUSIC SMARTS
by Mr. Bonzai
50449591 Book $14.99

MUSICIAN'S YOGA
by Mia Olson
50449587 Book $14.99

THE NEW MUSIC THERAPIST'S HANDBOOK – SECOND EDITION
by Dr. Suzanne B. Hanser
50449424 Book $29.95

HAL•LEONARD® CORPORATION
7777 W. BLUEMOUND RD. P.O. BOX 13819 MILWAUKEE, WI 53213

EAR TRAINING, IMPROVISATION, MUSIC THEORY

BEGINNING EAR TRAINING
by Gilson Schachnik
50449548 Book/CD $14.99

BERKLEE MUSIC THEORY – 2ND EDITION
by Paul Schmeling
50449615 Rhythm, Scales Intervals: Book/CD $24.99
50449616 Harmony: Book/CD $22.99

BLUES IMPROVISATION COMPLETE
by Jeff Harrington
Book/CD Packs
50449486 B♭ Instruments $19.95
50449488 C Bass Instruments $19.95
50449425 C Treble Instruments $22.99
50449487 E♭ Instruments $19.95

ESSENTIAL EAR TRAINING FOR THE CONTEMPORARY MUSICIAN
by Steve Prosser
50449421 Book $16.95

A GUIDE TO JAZZ IMPROVISATION
by John LaPorta
Book/CD Packs
50449439 C Instruments $19.95
50449441 B♭ Instruments $19.99
50449442 E♭ Instruments $19.99
50449443 B♭: Instruments $19.99

IMPROVISATION FOR CLASSICAL MUSICIANS
by Eugene Friesen with Wendy M. Friesen
50449637 Book/CD $24.99

REHARMONIZATION TECHNIQUES
by Randy Felts
50449496 Book $29.95

MUSIC BUSINESS

THE FUTURE OF MUSIC
by Dave Kusek and Gerd Leonhard
50448055 Book $16.95

HOW TO GET A JOB IN THE MUSIC INDUSTRY – 2ND EDITION
by Keith Hatschek
50449551 Book $27.95

MAKING MUSIC MAKE MONEY
by Eric Beall
50448009 Book $26.95

MUSIC LAW IN THE DIGITAL AGE
by Allen Bargfrede and Cecily Mak
50449586 Book $19.99

MUSIC MARKETING by Mike King
50449588 Book $24.99

THE SELF-PROMOTING MUSICIAN – 2ND EDITION
by Peter Spellman
50449589 Book $24.99

MUSIC PRODUCTION & ENGINEERING

FINALE: AN EASY GUIDE TO MUSIC NOTATION – 3RD EDITION
by Thomas E. Rudolph and Vincent A. Leonard, Jr.
50449638 Book $34.99

MIX MASTERS
by Maureen Droney
50448023 Book $24.95

PRODUCING & MIXING CONTEMPORARY JAZZ
by Dan Moretti
50449554 Book/DVD-ROM $24.95

PRODUCING AND MIXING HIP-HOP/R&B
by Mike Hamilton
50449555 Book/DVD-ROM $19.99

PRODUCING DRUM BEATS
by Eric Hawkins
50449598 Book/CD-ROM Pack $22.99

PRODUCING IN THE HOME STUDIO WITH PRO TOOLS – THIRD EDITION
by David Franz
50449544 Book/DVD-ROM $39.95

RECORDING AND PRODUCING IN THE HOME STUDIO
by David Franz
50448045 Book $24.95

UNDERSTANDING AUDIO
by Daniel M. Thompson
50449456 Book $24.99

SONGWRITING, COMPOSING, ARRANGING

ARRANGING FOR LARGE JAZZ ENSEMBLE
by Dick Lowell and Ken Pullig
50449528 Book/CD $39.95

COMPLETE GUIDE TO FILM SCORING – 2ND EDITION
by Richard Davis
50449607 ....$27.99

JAZZ COMPOSITION
by Ted Pease
50448000 Book/CD $39.99

MELODY IN SONGWRITING
by Jack Perricone
50449419 Book/CD $24.95

MODERN JAZZ VOICINGS
by Ted Pease and Ken Pullig
50449485 Book/CD $24.95

MUSIC COMPOSITION FOR FILM AND TELEVISION
by Lalo Schifrin
50449604 Book $34.99

MUSIC NOTATION
PREPARING SCORES AND PARTS
by Matthew Nicholl and Richard Grudzinski
50449540 Book $16.95

MUSIC NOTATION
THEORY AND TECHNIQUE FOR MUSIC NOTATION
by Mark McGrain
50449399 Book $24.95

POPULAR LYRIC WRITING
by Andrea Stolpe
50449553 Book $14.95

SONGWRITING: ESSENTIAL GUIDE
by Pat Pattison
50481582 Lyric and Form Structure: Book ...$16.95
50481583 Rhyming: Book $14.99

THE SONGWRITER'S WORKSHOP
by Jimmy Kachulis
50449519 Harmony: Book/CD $29.95
50449518 Melody: Book/CD $24.95

Prices subject to change without notice. Visit your local music dealer or bookstore, or go to www.berkleepress.com

1012

STUDY MUSIC
with
BERKLEE ONLINE

Study Berklee's curriculum, with Berklee faculty members, in a collaborative online community. Transform your skill set and find your inspiration in all areas of music, from songwriting and music production, to music business, theory, orchestration, and everything in between. Build lifelong relationships with like-minded students on your own time, from anywhere in the world.

Discover Your Own Path at
Berkleemusic.com

Learn On Your Own, But Never By Yourself